"LETTERS PRAY"

BY:

RICHARD A. GUTIÉRREZ

This book is dedicated to the One who got away, and to all the inmates at the Melton Crain Correctional Facility in Gatesville, Texas.

With much love and patience: read, write and create!

TABLE OF CONTENTS

Preface

I believe while we are all guilty of something, we should all strive towards innocence and recognize that there is goodness in everyone. People make mistakes which is an impetus that makes us human, and these mistakes are really lessons to be taught and learned to guide us in our future experiences and endeavors. The act of free-will gives us the ability to make choices, however volatile they appear to be at times, and character is built in those lessons but often times will-power is all we have to continue on.

Personal relationships are a great battleground to test your very limits of dedication, desire, and fortitude. The ups and downs of togetherness can help strengthen or weaken your alliance with a significant other and it can become an emotional roller coaster, and even a tug-of-war, that tugs on your heart strings. It is through communication when one can at least get a glimpse and continue to gauge if someone's intent is mal.

Deciphering and determining what are true and what is a lie, whether on purpose or not, is an acquired skill but intuition could play a significant part. The ability to understand something immediately, without the need for conscious reasoning, can be a valued asset in decision-making.

There were many factors involved in my decisions to write an inmate, and I learned several lessons in the process. There are a couple of important concepts to understand: First, *I* made initial contact and started the process of opening this Pandora's box. Secondly, *I* continued the conversation and had the best intentions on providing positivity and hope. Ultimately, I maintain my innocence in my relations with the inmate, as she was more than a "number" ...she was my friend.

Chapter 1:

Houston, Texas

It was towards the end of the 2015 school season, in May, and the children were anxious to be picked up by their family members or from official picker-uppers at the sound of the closing bell. The first to fifth graders were already lining up and being corralled by teachers and faculty members on this hot and humid afternoon, in Texas. Screaming and laughter surrounded the elementary school and echoed throughout the grounds. Doors opened and closed as the Safety Patrol kindly reunited the children to their respective vehicles, and teachers supervised the organized and efficient efforts that went into daily dismissal.

Pedro and I walked into the front doors and into the lobby looking for the Composition book that lays on the counter area by the receptionist. As quick as it took us to sign in, we about-faced out the front doors avoiding three young students who were happily playing a game of Tag. Our focus was directed towards the Portable building in the back area by the Track field, as we gripped our burlap bags filled with tools. We wore our grey uniformed shirts that displayed our first names, and matching grey caps accompanied by blue pants and steel-toed boots.

Strategizing our next efforts on maintaining the facility, inside an air-conditioned safe-haven, we sat on repaired and spare classroom chairs while on a mini-break, munching on Fritos and corn chips.

"What a day," I sighed.

"What a week! It's not even Summer and it's really super-hot out."

"Got to find a pool to jump in. What do you have planned for the weekend? I asked.

"I got the kids. Probably just stay home and watch some movies."

"Yeah, I got my Girls the following weekend. I've been thinking about visiting people at Senior Citizen Homes, tomorrow, just to say hi and hang out with them for a while."

"Why would you want to do that? Don't you have any projects you need to do around the house? Just sounds like a waste of time." he questioned.

I was crunching on the chips and took a swig of some Coke to wash it down, while I reminded myself on how I've been wanting to do this for quite some time. Both of my grandmothers were still alive living on the East Coast, but my grandfathers had already passed away. I was extremely lucky to have met them, as they were great men in my eyes and heart and I often wished that I got to know them better and spend quality time with them longer.

Family is very important to me and I had been apart from them for nearly five years because I transferred from Newark and moved to Houston to work for a major airline carrier. When that only lasted another five years, I began a new journey working for a school district in maintenance. I specialized in the pressure-washing department and found extreme joy working around elementary school children and periodically seeing my own girls in their classrooms, when I walk the hallways and peek in or visit during their lunch time.

Being a father to my two daughters had been my major focus in life and that was my role, my responsibility, my everything. I never gave up my love, protection and involvement in their lives and because they're really smart girls, they knew where I stood. After the divorce, the Attorney General constructed the terms and I became the non-custodial parent, with visitation, and as such, I became more familiar and involved with the Court system.

Perhaps I just wanted to be around those who either didn't have family anymore or didn't receive many, if any, visitors, but in any case, I felt compelled to give my spare time for the sake of another's happiness. Without explaining the entire motive to Pedro, I twisted the soda cap unto the finished bottle and looked at him.

"I think it'll be interesting and fun. I'll probably put a smile on someone's face." I asserted. "I'd even go visit random inmates in prisons for the same reason." I boldly stated.

"I don't know about that. Why don't you do what I did?" Pedro asked with a grin. He pulled out a picture of a girl from his wallet and slid it in front of me.

"Who is this?" I was bewildered.

"I met her on *WriteAPrisoner.com* and we've been talking for a few months now."

"What do you mean you met her?"

"We're pen pals and we just write back and forth," he explained.

Pen pals, huh? That wasn't a bad idea. I can just write to prisoners and it would be something to look forward to. There are too many people texting and, on their phones, and I think writing would be a cool way to communicate again.

I finished my chips and wiped my hands of the salt, then I pulled out my phone to check out this website. After logging on and researching, I found that there were numerous options and I could choose which profile, state, age or even gender from a multitude and plethora of candidates. *I was overwhelmed.* There were so many faces as I scrolled, but stopped at one in particular that caught my attention. She was also from Texas, had a pretty smile and wore glasses. That, and that she looked innocent enough, was a good start to get my thoughts flowing on what I actually wanted to do.

Break was over and I was eager to complete my duties so that I could write a warm and introductory letter to "Linda" which also meant pretty in Spanish. I was excited to start something new, to engage in an endeavor I only thought about doing and now I was to begin this new correspondence. But first, I had to rid of the grime and darkness that over-powered the school's walkways and the west side of their brick walls.

Moments after I pulled the starter cord to the engine, unwound the water hose and applied the powerful water pressure to the edifice, I thought about Linda while the brick transformed to a brighter red and the dirt was washing away to the nearest storm drain. I was motivated to embark on something new and pure. For me, this was an opportunity for a brand-new start to socialize on a hermit level, a sort of one-on-one interaction that I could hide and keep to myself. My intention was simple: To initiate contact with someone who, perhaps, was looking for a friend, or just someone to talk to. Like many new relationships, there is no real indication what the ultimate outcome would be, but I hoped for the best and prepared for the worst, so I definitely wanted to give it a try.

I kept thinking to myself - what do I write? How do I keep it friendly and neutral? But then I thought that I was thinking about it too much and that I should just be myself, however, I would be writing to a person in prison, a criminal charged through our Courts and now placed in our penal system. This isn't just saying hello to a random stranger at the local supermarket or mall. *Or was it?* What did I really know about the person deciding on which potato chips they were going to purchase? All I knew was that they were hungry and needed to consume, or that they just had the munchies. What would a person do to ultimately survive? At what great lengths would anyone perform for the sake of their personal gain and survival, and at what cost? Maybe I didn't think this through long enough, but it was just paper and pen, the cost of a stamp, and a little over a two-hundred-mile distance between us. A long-distance rapport combined with not seeing them equated to an ideal uncommitted relationship, and besides, ultimately, I am just wanting to be friends.

Pedro and I finished our work for the day and after putting away all of our tools and washing up, we met up at the newly cleaned yellow building with the comforting and cooling air conditioner and he took out his phone while I whipped out a pen and paper. Luckily, we finished just in time before the rain clouds came over us and it started to downpour. It was a perfect time to write.

Dear Linda,

Hi! How are you? My name is Coronado and I'm writing to you from Houston. I know we have two seasons here in Texas - hot & hotter, but right now it's raining so hard it's like a cow pissing on a flat rock. I'm just a regular guy who went on this website and found your info that was posted. Hope all is well with you! Here's my address if you'd like to write me back.

- Coronado

Because of personal and security reasons, I put my UPS Store mail box information, that I used for my side business. I was comfortable with that and, again, it kept a distance between me and this stranger. Trust is earned and I was cautious, if not for me but also for my daughters. I tried to take everything into consideration. Now, I put my intentions and letter out there and I just had to wait to see if she would reply.

CHAPTER 2:

Gatesville, Texas

Postmarked on 02 JUN 2015

Dear Coronado,   *5-31-15*

I am writing you in reply to Linda's letter. She is my very best friend and we have been very close thru this time we have done in prison. She found your letter very precious and she was touched by your compassion. But she is very overwhelmed with responses right now. She did not want to leave you with an unanswered letter. So, she asked me if I would like to write you. She believes that everyone needs someone and she felt we would be good for each other. I am very happy and excited to also have someone to write.

Now I would like to tell you a little about myself. My name is Bonnie Wright, I am white and 37 years old. I am 5'4" and weigh about 140lbs. I have hazel eyes and blondish brown hair that goes to my waist. I was raised in the country, so I am a country girl, but choose to live a lot of my life in the city. I love the peacefulness of the country and being able to view God's creation. I love the city because I love to shop and find fun activities to do with my family. In the summer I love to be outside but in the winter I hide out indoors. I do not like being cold! I spend my time reading and watching movies, anything that will allow me to be indoors and I can stay warm. I am not sure what all you would like to know about me so I will leave it up to you to ask questions. My life is an open book. My story is very long and difficult in areas but I am not ashamed of it. Through it I have learned so much and I am a better person because of it. I'm here on a Burglary of a Habitation because of a 3-year drug habit. I have an 18-year sentence and I have almost 3 years done on it. I see parole in October and pray to be home by the end of this year. Well, that's most of my Story and I look forward to hearing about you. I am not on a website and won't be because it's too expensive. I also know you would like to put a face to the name so I'm working on getting copies for you. I would also like one (photo) of you, not that looks matter, it's what's on the inside that counts. I will be waiting for your reply. It's always wonderful to get a ray of sunshine in the midst of this dark place. I hope this letter brightens your day and brings you much joy.

Sincerely,
Bonnie

I could not believe it! When I checked my mailbox a couple of days later, I received this letter from a woman, other than Linda, and it confused me. I thought that maybe something was terribly wrong, or that Linda was already released and the Warden, or someone from their administration, wrote to me to explain the situation. The Christina Melton Crain Unit is a Texas Department of Criminal Justice prison for females in Gatesville, Texas, and I made contact. When I exited the UPS Store I immediately went into my car, locked the doors and cranked the air-conditioner back up again, and after I carefully opened the envelope, I slowly began reading her letter.

When I went to work the next day, I told Pedro all about it during lunch. He told me about *JPay* and how they are committed to helping friends and family stay connected to incarcerated loved ones through a variety of corrections-related services, and also providing quick and reliable payment options for individuals in community corrections. It was the company that offered a fast and secure method of sending money to prisoners, for a fee. He guided me through the process since he was talking with Tina from the same Unit. It was pretty straight-forward so I opened an account, sent her a *JPay* email and attached a photo of myself to it. The inmates would get the copy printout from the corrections officers.

I also immediately wrote her back, amazed on how this concept had been given life and I wanted to continue the momentum of our newfound friendship. Because of my faith in the Universe, I believed that things happened for a reason and that Bonnie was meant to be in my life as my new pen pal. I also believed in intention and free will, and whatever it was that was occurring I enjoyed it but still had my reservations. I told her that it was an opportunity for us to begin a new start, free to be ourselves, and to write about anything we wanted to. It didn't matter that I did not know what she looked like, because, as she said, "it's what's on the inside that counts". In the letter I told her about my new findings, opportunities and suggested that I even go visit her. It didn't take long for me to drop that letter in the mail.

Good day, Bonnie!   *8:15am*

Hope this email finds you well. I already sent a reply letter which I hope you'll receive by today. :-) I wanted to surprise you plus get your opinion on something. I may be visiting Central TX over the weekend. Are you able to have Contact visits? I may be overstepping my bonds and I don't want to interfere with your plans, but since I might be in your neighborhood I wanted to know if I could stop over. Read my letter, check my pic first and let me know. Lol! Remember, it's what's in the inside that counts :-p If so, let me know in your return letter... Have a Fantastic Day!!

- Coronado

Postmarked on 11 JUN 2015

Dear Coronado,   *6-10-15*

   Wow! I can tell this is going to work out really well. When I got your letter, I was like this "freakin' guy"! I have heard from you more than I have heard from anyone this month. That is really awesome! I want to thank you for this because you will never know how much I needed this. You are truly great! I got your letter and J-Pay today and was very excited to get back in touch with you. You know all things happen for a reason. So, I am excited to see where this will all go. I wanted to tell you that it is a beautiful thing that you want to come visit because I would love that more than anything. But we have certain ways we have to do things. We can only add or remove people on our visiting list every 6 months. That will be next month but until then we can get to know each other thru mail or phone calls. You can have your phone registered if you call 1-866-806-xxxx. If it's a cell phone it has to be a contract, no pre-paid. If you choose to do this, we could be talking in about 3 days I believe! Not too sure so you will have to check on that. Now, with the mail I will always write you back but I need you to know that I have 5 wonderful children that I write to often. They don't live in the same homes so I don't always have a lot of stamps. I will have to put them first as any mother would but you will be right under them. Believe me if I had enough stamps, I would write all the time. I love to write. So, you will always have plenty to read. I will always let you know when I'm running low on stamps so you will not be left wondering what happened. My family is very supportive of me and help me when they can but they can't always do for me. And that is o.k. I do the best with what I got. I want to tell you about my children because they are my world. Raul is my oldest son. He is 21 years old. He is also in prison. That's a hard pill to swallow! We are not here on the same charge. We grew up together and had a hard life. Casey is my only daughter. She is 19 years old and lives with her grandmother. She is so much like me! My middle son is Gabriel. He's 15 years old and he lives with his father. My youngest two are full brothers and live together. Jack is 13 yrs. old and John is 10 yrs. old. They all do have different dads except the youngest two. I've had a hard life and spent my life going from one man to another looking for love but only finding abuse and heart ache. Then it led to drugs to numb the pain, which led me here. And I thank the Lord for bringing me here to give me a second chance at life. My children are very supportive and are involved in my life as much as they can. Only thru letters. I have only had one visit in 2 ½ yrs. and that was this April. My Mom, Brother and middle son, Gabriel came. Just a little history for you to go by.

I see that your family is from Puerto Rico. It truly surprises me because I seem to get along with y'all very well. Do you have a Jersey accent or a Puerto Rican one? I was born in Andrews, TX and raised in the Lubbock area and my mother is in the Amarillo area. I have lived mostly around my mother but have been all over Texas. My life's been a very long and hard journey but now I'm ready to live life.

I have to say I loved your photo and I am very excited to get more. I only have one photo of myself and I'm sending it to get copies. My family won't send me any of myself. I've tried. I have many on my Facebook if you are able to see them. I'm from Memphis, TX. You might can look me up. But as soon as I get it back, I will have you one in the mail. What would be even more awesome is if you could come visit on a weekend, they'll take pictures and we could have one taken together! :-) Just an idea!

What I miss the most is holding my babies. I miss them very much. I miss spending time with them and just having fun. I enjoy making the most of every moment. I believe making good memories are the key to a happy life. My favorite food is??? I love food! All kinds of food. What I would love to eat right now is a salad! Yummy!

My favorite color is green but like any girl, I like pink. When I get out, I want to get on my feet. I can go to my mothers and my brothers and do that. They will help me as much as they can. They don't understand anything about getting back into the real world after being in Prison, so they will struggle with how to help. I can do it but I will need support. I love horses and living in the country. It has become a goal of mine to start a prison ministry when I get out. I believe if I keep coming back to help others in here, I have hope it will keep me reminded not to come back. I want to give back what someone gave me! I do love the Lord but it's nothing I throw on others. My favorite book is the Bible because it has the best stories in the world. You can give me a big hug any time you want to. But the first real one will be when you come to visit. Like I said, ask all the questions you would like because I am an open book. Really, I have nothing to hide. I think you are a very sweet and handsome man. I feel your compassion for others and I see that you are willing to share it with someone who will give some in return. I have a very big heart and I want everyone to be happy. I'm one of those who will find a way to turn things around for the sad or lonely. But a lot of the times I'm that person that's sad or lonely. You have truly brightened my life in a major way! :-p So, thank you very much! I have been thinking about you a lot the last

8

two days, wondering when I would hear from you and if you would ever care to write me back. So, it was a burst of sunshine when I got my mail today!

I would have loved to have been sitting next to you fishing this weekend. We would have had a lot of fun. Well, did you catch anything? It's great that you are an outdoors person. I spend a lot of time outside here. I walk or run around the track or sit at the tables and look in the sky. I do a lot of soul searching because I need to find the areas of my life that are missing something or that need something removed. I can say I am not the same person when I came in. Sometimes your beliefs and values get messed up and you have to stop long enough to see they are messed up and fix them. I have overcome so much in this place! Now I don't like being here one bit but it has been life changing.

Well, my heart is overwhelmed with excitement to hear back from you. So, I'm going to get this in the mail. I also want you to get this before you try to come because they won't let you in. You're so amazing for that and I hope you get down this way when I can get you on my list! Write me and let me know more about you. Do you have children? What's your favorite color and food? Do you have a hobby and what do you do for a living? What do you do in your spare time besides write me now? I'm going to get this in the mail. Hope this has made your day as much as you have made mine. I can't wait to hear back!

Sincerely,
Bonnie

P.S.

Look...I don't know what it is but I am going to go out on a limb here and send you the <u>only</u> picture I have of me & my daughter. This means more to me than diamonds or gold, so please make sure I get this back. You can make copies of it but please send this one back ASAP! For some reason I trust you. I want you to know who you are talking to and I know you would never not return this. We look so much a like except she is half Mexican and has dark hair. Please return her to me soon! :p

Bonnie sent me a photograph of herself and her daughter, parked in the front seat of a vehicle. They both looked so happy and their gleaming teeth and big smiles were contagious enough for me to smile back at it, in excitement. These were two beautiful young ladies and I shared in their projected joy.

I hope you like books because I just wrote you one! LOL!

Coronado,   *6-18-15*

I hope this letter finds you doing great. I wanted to write a little after our phone call today. I think it is really amazing that you have gone all out to make it where we can have constant contact. What's more amazing is that you drove here and went thru so much to see me. That shows me that you are not afraid of new things and are willing to go the extra mile for others. In here you learn to cherish the smallest things in life. And being able to pick up a phone and have contact with someone in the free world is a great thing. And to have a conversation with someone who doesn't even know you but cares enough to get to know you is a very beautiful thing to me.

Now I haven't gotten your letter and I'm sure it will answer a lot of my questions, but one thing I am curious about is what you are looking for in all of this. I don't want you to take this just any way but I want to make you as happy as you make me! So, I need to know more about what you want from me. Do you need more letters in the mail other than the reply to your letters? What could I do to make your life easier and more enjoyable? To be truthful with you this is all so unbelievable. For someone who has not had much contact with others to having it all in about a week. I'm truly amazed! My mind seems to be having a hard time processing all of this. I have come to believe you might be an angel sent straight from heaven. I'm very excited to get to know you better.

I am very sorry you had a wasted trip here but I am so glad it was a good experience. My mind is blown away that you would even come so soon. I love that about you. You're not afraid to do new things or take a good risk to meet someone new. Even someone with a past like myself. You have to be an angel! I say all this because my mother has only written me 2 letters the whole time I have been locked up. My daughter doesn't have contact with me. Her grandmother wants me to let me know how she is. My three youngest children write me a few times a year but not as much as I would like. My father writes about 4 times a year and my other two brothers and sister only write about every couple of months and they all update me about everything in one J-Pay. So, I don't get much mail. I know that they love me dearly and miss me very much. They just don't understand how lonely it gets here. They don't have the phone hooked up and probably won't. I have had the one visit that was amazing. They really don't understand how all this works and I don't think they really want to know. It hurts them so much that I am here. So, it's like out of sight out of mind. And that's ok because I am tired of hurting them. I put myself here and I will have to be the one to get me out. So, this is all a big change but it's a great change! I am very grateful for all of this. You have truly given me a new sense of hope and made my time here a lot happier. I wanted to answer some of your questions real fast before I start rambling on. Ok the marriage thing gets a little difficult but nothing I can't take care of when I get out. I was married 22 years ago to my oldest son's father. I lived with him for only a year and I've never seen him again. I found his family about 10 years later and found out he had married again twice so I thought I was divorced from him. So about 7 years ago I married a different man but later found out I was never divorced from the first. It has been really crazy but I don't wish to be married to either of them. So, I will get a divorce from the first which will void out the second. I can get 2 divorces at one time. I don't have any children from my second one. He is the one who introduced me to meth. So now that is answered, let's move on. I told you my life is very difficult. I have a lot of messes to clean up when I get out. I do have 4 very special men in my life and they are my boys. Other than that, I have no one. But of course, you now! I have 3 tattoos, my first husband's name on my left hand between my thumb and first finger and my second husband's name on my ring finger. I have a mess of a tattoo on my lower back. It was one of those times when I shouldn't have been getting a tattoo, but I did and woke up the next day wondering what was on my back. It's very bad! LOL! I did have my nose, belly button, tongue and my ears all pierced. But now of course I don't have any because they have all closed up. I'm not really sure if I will get them redone when I get out. I'm believe I'm getting too old for them. I don't know. What do you think? I love it that you have two children. And girls at that! I only have one girl but always wanted more. I do need you to know this...I have 5 of my own children that I gave birth to but I have a step-daughter and two step-sons I have raised most of their lives and they are also very much a part of my life. I had my hands full with all of them but loved every part of being a mother. They were very active in all events and I was a very attentive parent in all they did. Ok back to your letter. I love food and all different kinds. I also love to cook so spending time in the kitchen would be great. But that means I will also have to work out a lot more. I would love to try new foods and also learn how to cook them. You can teach me all you know! But you also have to be willing to let me teach you. I love change and new things are a plus for me. I would like to see some of the work you do on canvas. I enjoy art! You should see some of the art they do in here. It's really amazing. I'm excited for you that you will be completing your degree in Aug. Maybe one day you could paint a portrait of me! What do you think? Would I have to sit still for a long period of time? I don't know if I can do that. I have to be constantly moving. My mom says I have the "gogo's". I believe if you're not busy that it gives room for Satan to come in and control your thoughts. So, I keep my mind busy which in turn leads to my body being busy. When I read your letters, I see that you're very eager to get up here to meet me! That is really exciting. I might not know how to act to be meeting with

11

someone I've never known. I will be o.k. because I'm a people person. We do get to have contact visits. We do get to hug when we first come in and when we leave. I do believe we can hold hands across the table from each other. You know the visit really depends on the officers that work that day. Some are very nosey and others are very laid back. They may ask you questions like how you know me and how long you have known me and you don't have to answer all those questions. They are just trying to find out something to talk about. For real if they asked me, I would tell them it wasn't any of their business. In a nice, respectful way but I would let them know they are over-stepping their boundaries. I don't have anything to hide but they are in our business enough that I feel something I should be able to keep to myself. We can take pictures once a month. So, I will be sure to let you know what day it will be so you can come on that day. You can put your arm around and we can take them standing. The touching has to be done in a respectful way for, one, in respect of each other and, two, there are other families in there. You will for sure get your chance to hug me and hold my hand. Kissing is also allowed but I don't believe we are there yet! I submitted a form to see when I can change my visiting list so I will let you know when I find out. About the photo I sent you, I haven't changed a whole lot. I'm sure I weighed more there. I promise you will not be disappointed. I will make myself look really nice for you! My daughter does look a lot like me and acts a lot like me also. I have to keep her in my prayers often! Sometimes it's a great thing and others it's not good at all. I wish we had a better relationship but we have a rough past. It's a bitter sweet story, with lots of bumps and breaks. Long story and maybe one day I will get a chance to tell you.

I see you talk about being active in your family's lives so I wonder why you went to an all-boys school. Was it a private school they paid to send you to? Did your sister Gloria go to an all-girls school? I always went to a public school so I don't know much about it. I do know it was a religious school. Here's some good information about me, I am a Preacher's Daughter! He and my mother divorced when I was 4 and he stepped down. He then became absent from my life for most of my life. He has just begun to become part of my life. Because I decided that I needed that part of my life to be complete in order for me to start to fix the things that had been broken in me because of his absence. So, are you a part of your daughters' lives? I bet you are an awesome Daddy! And on this note I would like to wish you a very Happy Father's Day! I just spent the last few days sending out cards to my Dad, Brothers and son for Father's Day. So, let me tell you how I am a little low on stamps. That's why I'm also trying to get as much as I can in this letter. We always have the phone! My family only sends me certain amounts of money a month and I have to make it last. So, bear with me please. They just sent me some a couple of weeks ago and I had to buy a lot of stuff because they didn't have it to send the two months before then. But it's o.k. I have learned to make it. O.K. enough about that! My favorite music is Christian music off of Air One (it's a radio station)! But I also love country. I will listen to all kinds of music though. I also like to dance, can't wait to be your partner. When can we start? I guess I got to get me out of here first. On that note one thing that has been going thru my mind is, were you looking to meet someone about to be released or are you willing to do this as long as needed? You know just one of those things a girl would like to know. Me and Linda were talking earlier and she wanted me to let you know that I am much happier and have a little more pep in my step since we have begun talking. She wanted you to know that she is glad it has worked out great for the both of us. She is very excited to see how this thing turns out! She's my best friend, we do everything together! We work together, live together, we are in choir together, we workout together, we do it all together! I thank her so much for making our connection.

So, tell me a little bit about why you want to start over new in your life? Has something happened in your life that has made you make the choice? I know that in my life there has been two major events in my life that caused me to change how I lived. So, I am sure something has triggered this change. If you don't want to talk about it that's o.k. too. Mine was when an 8yr abusive relationship ended and I lost who I was and was introduced to meth. That was the beginning of losing my life and coming to prison has allowed me to find myself and slowly began to gain my life back. This was a difficult but life-changing event for me. I am thankful for it because it has allowed me to grow in ways I would never have without being here. This has not been all bad experiences, there have been less bad than good. I have had a chance to accomplish so much and in an environment where I could do it without all the distraction that life out there brings. I have to say I am content and safe here. I want to go home more than you could ever imagine but I know that my time will come when it comes.

You know I was sitting here I thought for a moment I could hear you singing outside my window! I was thinking... "this freakin' guy!" The way you have been making things happen I'm not sure you couldn't make it happen! You're a truly awesome guy! I can't understand why you are divorced. I have never had a man come thru the way you have but my picker has been broken all of my life. You know at some point you figure out that you need to stop and let someone else do the picking!

Well, I will tell you a little about my day then I will end this book I have wrote you. I told you I love to write. Oh, and I have to say I love it that you write me random stuff like that. I am the same way! So, it's been raining off and on for days now. We don't usually get up until about 7:30 or 8:00 on our days off and we kind of do our own thing. I read the Bible and do my devotionals and spend some time with the Lord. We go to lunch (also known as chow) about 10:00. After that we go walk around the track or sit outside and talk. We have count time at 12:30 so we have to be in for that. About 1:15 count clears and we can go back out. So, we go workout. Let me tell you I

13

worked out so hard today that I busted a hole in the side of my shoe. That's some working out! Lol! Then we get ready to come in and the rain decides to pour. So, when I get in, I am a soaked little puppy. I was going to go to dinner at about 3:00 but I just skipped it because I wanted to get out of those clothes. Then I got your letter and I had to come sit down so I could see what was happening in your life. After such a trying day I needed a ray of sunshine to get me thru.

You always come thru right on time. I'm not real sure when you will get this because you weren't clear on when you were going to your parents. Come get me and I will go with you! I'm sure you could work some kind of a deal! No, you have a great time and I'm sure you will hear from me before you get this. Oh, one more thing I'm not into taking advantage of anything or anyone. So, at any point any of this becomes too much for you let me know. And about the phone calls I am o.k. with a couple of calls a week. Not that I don't want to talk to you it's just I know things cost money and I'm not the one to overstep anything. So, don't do more than you are comfortable with. I will only call when you tell me to. Anything that you do I want you to do it because you want to, I don't ever want to become a burden to you in any way. Thank you dearly for all that you have already done. You will never know what a difference you have made in my life. I'm going to go get this in the mail and get some sleep. You are in my thoughts all the time and in my prayers. Have a wonderful Father's Day! Your pictures were great! How can you still be a single man? I don't get it, you're very nice looking! Have sweet dreams!

Sincerely,
Bonnie

P.S.

Can't wait to hear back from you. Those 20 min phone calls don't allow much time, so you're going to have to write me also.

Dearest Coronado,   *6-19-15*

How is your morning? Mine has been wonderful. I just went to go eat lunch (at 10:00 in the morning) and we had some veggies we don't even get to have. They were amazing! It was corn on the cob and cucumbers with Ranch. That sounds like a great meal to eat first thing in the morning doesn't it? Lol! It was so good! Now I'm sitting here without much to do, so I was thinking about you. Wondering how you start your day. It's one of those rainy days here! Real cloudy and wet. Just really bored today! So how is your day going? I'm sure there is rain there if the storm hasn't already passed. You really made my day yesterday when you spoke about you and your girls were talking about me. I would love to know more about them and the things they like. As you know I love children and love to do things that are fun with them. I would love to send them cards and things that would make their days brighter, if that is O.K. It's really exciting to be a part of a whole other family's lives. I would love to see a photo of you and your girls. I have photos of my children that I could send you so you could put a face to their names. You would have to send them back of course! I might just get some out to send with this letter! Well, those were just some random thoughts for the day. I am going to go get ready for church. I'll write more later!

6-22-15

I know it's been a few days since I've written but I have talked on the phone to you <u>a lot</u> these last couple of days. That has been amazing. And I loved talking to your girls! So, I'm up early this morning to go to work and he has never called us out. But I had gotten behind on my Bible College so I got this all caught up. Thank goodness because I'm not one to let myself get behind. I believe in getting things done ahead of time to leave room for other things that might come up. I would also rather be early than late. But I have also learned that its's o.k. for things not to go the way you plan them. So, I was here wondering what are some of your dreams or fears? What are some of those things that strike a nerve with you? You seem to be a very calm and gentle person but I know everyone has a bad side, so what brings that out in you? What are some things that you enjoy others to do for you or with you? People that I care about, I like them to spend time with me. It's wonderful when they buy me things but I would rather make memories than have tons of things. Before I thought I had to have the newest everything and dress the best. Now that I have lost all of that, I can see that never made me happy in the first place. I have lived with very little when growing up but also had more than I needed when I got out on my own. I've spent most of my life gathering up things that never made me happy. So now I want to live the rest of my life just living. My question is what is life really about? I intend to find

15

out! Well, I did some checking and I can add you on the 11th of July and it only takes three days to process it. So, you should be good to go by the weekend of the 18th if you would like to come! I would really like to know if you're coming so I could have a chance to get dressed! If not, they want us coming out the way we are. I don't want to have just gotten done working out and then call me! LOL! Oh, and don't make fun of me because they make us wear these clothes here that are too big on us. I'm not trying to be gangsta, it's just what they give us. I tell the girls here that I'm wearing my Dad's pants because they are SO BIG! It doesn't bother me too much because I don't get caught up in the times of this place. This is only for a moment. Well, I'm going to go outside for a little while before they want to count us again! That's one thing I won't ever miss is being counted! LOL! I pray your day has been as blessed as mine has been. More so now that you're in it! I just got off the phone with you and felt like something was not right. I'm not sure if you had a bad day or if you were distracted while you were eating. So of course, I have to call you back. These are the moments I lose all my hardness. Because I know everyone has bad days but I will have to do anything in the world to make it better. So, I have to call back and make sure you have the best night even if your day wasn't so great. You know I have to wait for me to get counted before I can get out there to you. I need you to know that you can talk to me about anything. You don't have to worry about offending me. I will let you know how I feel about things but you will never run me off. It doesn't take me long to get comfortable with people because I love meeting new people and helping in any way possible. If I had the money, I would send you a letter every day just to make you smile. You just really have to let me know things you would like for me to do. Let me be bold!! My feelings are getting involved but I also know that I have to take things slow because I've not made great choices in my past and that has resulted in me being very hurt. I don't have walls up but I do have boundaries. I want to get to know everything about you and then if things go well, then it's good. I really think you are amazing. I'm not going to tell you what you want to hear if it's not truly how I feel. I will tell you I feel very comfortable with you at this point. Maybe more so than you. But it's o.k. I also got your letter and I love how you pay close attention to details. I like that! I am the same way. If someone is lying, I will figure it out. I don't do it on purpose, it's just how I am. So, I like it that you're that way also. You talked about family and I want you to know that God comes first and then my family. That's all I have ever wanted is a loving, caring, and respectful husband and a house full of kids! I got the kids but never could find the husband. Look, I understand it couldn't be all of them because it wasn't. I'm a big reason nothing ever worked out. I had a lot of issues I was carrying around. I was one that would get close to you but then when you got too close, I would push you away because I didn't want you to hurt me so I would cause a break to protect myself. I thought I was protecting myself but it was destructive behavior that caused me lots of heartache. So now I want to just be normal and find out what happens when someone gets too close. I just pray that God will send *me the perfect one who can deal with me! LOL! I'm hard to deal with sometimes. I like to get my way and can be a little spoiled sometimes but this place has pretty much broke me out of that! Man, that was one thing I wanted to hold on to. Well, I'm going to go call you!*

O.K. I'm better knowing you are better! You're such an awesome guy, Coronado. I feel you're coming out of your shell so much more and this is going to be great. I really need you to come see me on the 18th of July. Oh, and I won't be knocking anyone off of my list that will ever come see me. So, no worries about that. Hey, look I want you to be free to be you. I want you to be comfortable being you around me. I have never been more me around any as I have around you. I'm not playing or joking around about that. What you see is what you get. My kids and family have not even had a chance to know this me! So be free to be you! It's really an awesome feeling. Oh, Linda told me to let you know that you will have to pay the phone bill soon or it will restrict it on my end. You call the same # you called to hook it up she said. So, if I don't call at some point it's because of the bill not being paid + it's restricted for me. I just want to let you know so if this happens you won't think it's because I don't want to. It's because I can't! I will probably freak out! I like it when I need to hear your voice, I can pick up the phone! So, check on that please! O.K. back to your letter, about the kids. I love them all to pieces. Raul – I was 17yrs old when I had him and Casey – I was 19yrs old. So, we grew up together, you could say. I can say that I have a pretty good relationship with all of my kids' fathers. I'm not saying they don't say things about me to the kids but I know they make sure I hear from them and get photos. We may disagree about things but we can always come to some sort of agreement. They have been very supportive thru my addiction and me coming to prison. Not once have they kept them from me. I'm sure when I get out down the line the youngest three will be back with me. They are ready for mom to come home.

6-23-15

O.K., had to go to work today and it was a really long and humid day. Got off work in time to shower and get to Bible College. Almost couldn't stay awake thru the whole class. Came in and got my mail and you made me cry. You made my whole day! I tried to call but it was late! You are truly amazing and I am very grateful to have you in my life. I am really at a loss for words. I am in awe of you and this whole situation. I am going to get this in the mail. Just know I am blessed.

Sincerely,
Bonnie

It was in this letter that I noticed a small slip of paper in the envelope. It was to be the first of many, and it signified that the Correctional Facility opened and perhaps read the contents. For the sake of tracking which letters were affected I wrote a "GIC" after the postmark date.

GIC: GENERAL INMATE CORRESPONDENCE * TEXAS DEPARTMENT OF CRIMINAL JUSTICE – INSTITUTIONAL DIVISION   *I-290 (07/93)

Postmarked on 29 JUN 2015   GIC

My Coronado,   *6-25-15*

I was just sitting here thinking about you, and decided to drop you a few lines on paper! I hope your week has been great! As for me it has been very long and tiresome. But I get a 3-day weekend so I should get caught up on my rest. So, I have been thinking about something and it has been bothering me. I feel like if I don't say it then I will go crazy! You remember when you said for me to only call every other day and now, I call every day and sometimes twice a day. Well, this is how I feel, when I call, I feel like I'm taking advantage of that. I don't want to overuse that because there might be a time when I will really need to get a hold of you and can't. Believe me I would talk to you all day every day if I could but I know these calls aren't free. I also feel that if you hadn't already thought it thru and knew what you wanted to budget these calls you wouldn't have said so in the beginning. So, when I call, I feel like I'm breaking our rule and when I don't call, I feel guilty because I know you put aside that time every day to talk to me then I don't call. So, we got to clear this up. I have learned to follow rules and really feel like I'm overstepping this! O.K. I'm done! I loved the pictures of you and the girls, they are beautiful! You are a really good daddy! It looks like y'all have so much fun together! I want to go with y'all! So, I got your letter and I love that you are a true romantic. I love how you spell your feelings out on paper. I want you to be able to talk to me about anything. I'm here to help you and listen. But I also need for you to know that I have been locked up for about 3yrs and I have not had this kind of relationship with anyone in that long. So, you have to be easy with me and let me crawl into this. I've had a not so great past and a lot of things have happened to me. So, when I get triggered it takes me a minute to sort thru my feelings. What I need you to do is hold my hand and walk me thru this. You haven't done anything wrong, it's just old feelings and emotions I haven't dealt with yet. So that being said you cannot be acting all crazy when you come to see me! I know it may be hard to keep your hands off of me but you can't be doing that or they will stop our visit! I know it's going to be hard to contain yourself but you have to if you want to

18

come back! Oh, and we have razors here so there ain't no hairy snatch. We must get that straight! She's clean cut! Now that we got that out of the way let's move on. I can't believe I'm talking to you about that! LOL! I just had to address that. Please forgive me! I am very grateful to have you in my life. I really like talking to you and getting to know you. I love your art work. That was very nice. You did that! I would like it if you would paint me something some time (when I get out). What pose would be the best? I would prefer to be dressed not no Titanic poses right yet! Remember take things slowly! LOL! Oh, random: I have to tell you this before I forget they only take pictures once a month. On the first of the month. In July it's on the 5th & in Aug. it's on the 1st. So, you will have to wait for forever to get our picture taken. That really sucks but it will pass by fast. I'm glad to be here for as long as it takes because I'm sure burnt out on some of the timing of some of the people in my life. I know we will get to a point sooner or later where everything will pan out but it doesn't have to stop. OK? You know you get that a lot in here. Even from family. I know life gets busy out there but I feel like sometimes they just forget about me. I mean I guess it's alright they didn't put me in here! Let me get off that subject! It can just feel like you're lost in here sometimes. I was lost but now I'm found! So much on that note, I have heard the story of God's rescue and I'm jumping on the first ride I can get. And thank you for being here to help me. You're really a special person in my life. You make me really feel good and I'm very comfortable talking to you. I also am at ease sharing things about my family with you. Trust me I don't do that a lot. I already had you looking on Facebook and everything! WOW! That's a big step for me and I didn't even think twice about it. O.K. Now about my parole...I pray and believe in my heart that I will get a favorable parole answer. I have done everything and more that they have asked me to do. I stay very involved in anything that will help me better myself. I have asked my family and friends to write me support letters to send in. I hope they have you know I can do everything humanly possible but God has the last word. I feel pretty sure I have got this one. So, this can be a start to your prayer life. Please pray for me as I'm always praying for you and the girls. Everyone is seeing them about 3 months early, so I have a good chance to see them next month! Yeah! I have almost 100 certificates to give to them and I've sent in my own parole letter. I know God has a plan and a purpose for my life and it's not in here as an inmate. It might be as a teacher or such. I know what has been spoken over me and I believe all of it will come to pass. It's bigger than me so I know it has to come from something bigger than me. The devil wants for me to be afraid of it but fear is not of God, I just have to know that it's not me but Christ that lives in me that will accomplish it all. Romans 8:28 God works all things out for the good for those who love him and are called according to his purpose. I know I love him more than anything and I know I have been called according to His purpose. So, He will work all things out for my good! I could write you for days about this. This is one thing I am passionate about. I have an amazing testimony. I know you have said you have fallen away and the first step back is just *doing it. You know what the word says so you have to just get back in it and watch it become real and alive. I will do what I can to help you. That's a promise! Well, it's late and I'm writing by just the moon lite and it's getting hard to see. I was going to get up early in the morning and mail this but I've got more to say. Hey look you will never know how amazing it makes me feel to know I can count on you to have me something in the mail all the time. You are more than I ever asked for. You know God will give you the desires of your heart but it's always more than you ask for. You have been more of a friend than most of my friends. Sweet Dreams and good night!*

6-27-15

Today is the day I called to talk to you knowing you would make my day brighter. But come to find out you were having one also. I'm very sorry you didn't make it in time to take your test. I'm sure if it was because we're both in our feelings today but something you said really hit me hard. I also absolutely <u>hate</u> ending the phone call on the note we have been here lately. First of all, when we end our calls on a not so great level, it leaves me sitting over here feeling guilt or upset about something that was said. I don't have a phone to pick up and call someone else or a TV to turn to watch ever to get my mind off of things. I have to sit here and think about things. I know maybe I shouldn't care enough to worry about it but I do. I have hurt a lot of people in my life and my goal in life is to encourage others and help them heal from past hurts but not to the point I get hurt. So, I would guess by now you would have to know I got my feelings a little hurt. I think it's more because of how the issue came up. For one you compared what your ex-wife did to what my charge is. It would have been a lot easier if you would have just asked me how I got my charge. I'm going to tell you because I'm not here to hide anything from you. I have no reason to. I was on drugs pretty bad right before this and was trying to get away from it. My friend which became my boyfriend was in my life helping me. I was a very bad junkie but I was always clean with it. I had lost everything at this time including my home, children, job and degree. So, I was down and out but I knew I didn't want to live that way anymore. I went thru some major withdrawals at that time and some serious pain. It was hard to hold down a full-time job, so I moved in with my sister. She didn't have a job and she has two children. My youngest brother had a firewood cutting business and we were all working for him to make ends meet and it wasn't enough. On this day the kids came in from school and were hungry and there was nothing in the house to eat. I mean nothing, and we had no money. So, my sister was out with her boyfriend and he was a serious thief and was on drugs something awful. My daughter was wanting to run around with them but I didn't want her to because I didn't want her in trouble. Anyways I was going down to my sister-in-law's to get something from her to feed the kids but it had gotten late and they were asleep. I could have gotten *something out of their freezer outside but I didn't have their go-ahead so I didn't. So, we drove to the rundown shack that my sister's boyfriend was living in. When we got there, he was rolling up some cords on drills and saws and we asked him where he had gotten them from because we knew they weren't his. He said the same place where he was going to get some guns and we asked where. He said across the street. Well, my uncle that was in the nursing home lived there. So, I was pissed! So not thinking I went over to check what all was missing and found they had already been in his house. My daughter was with me at this time as a friend. I was not high at the time but I didn't want to have any involvement with the cops. I will just say that there were many guns taken from the home and I'm not sure of all that I was charged with but I will say I didn't have any of what was taken in my possession at any time. My boyfriend and I were charged for this because my daughter was angry with me the next day because I didn't want her around my sister's boyfriend so she called the cops on me. I wanted her to stay at home or she would have to stay at her dad's. Her father and I haven't really gotten along and he always took her side. Of course he would that's his daughter. It was such a bad deal, me and my boyfriend left for the weekend to go spend it with his parents for his birthday. I didn't know at the time my daughter, her dad, my sister, her boyfriend & my mom had all gotten together and turned us in. They all took her side because I had been messed up on drugs and hadn't been doing right. They couldn't believe I would ever be really doing right. I can't blame them. We were arrested in Amarillo, TX where his family lives at my best friend's house. She knew they had a warrant for my arrest and called me in. So, me and my boyfriend went to jail, they took my car and searched it. I never was sure why I was in there for a few days. I spent 51 days in County jail and my daughter would come every weekend, her and my sister. Until a couple of weeks passed and my daughter wouldn't come and my sister finally told me it was because she was the one who turned me in and that she was sorry and she didn't want me to hate her. When I found out, nothing else mattered but getting on to hold my baby and let her know she couldn't do anything so bad I would hate her or not love her. I got out on 5yrs deferred probation a couple of days before Christmas and things were great. Until a few major issues happened to me and my children that is still hard to talk about. I was out 10 months and used once to help ease the pain, I thought. My probation officer did a hair strain test on me and it came back positive. They revoked me and put me back in County. Within 2 ½ months I was sitting in TDCJ. My boyfriend got 8yrs deferred probation, had 8 positive drug tests, they sent him to rehab and is free. He has been to prison 5 other times. I know I have $3,000.00 of restitution to pay back for all that was taken and they divided it between us. I just found this out when I went to see parole last year. My son said there were 8 guns missing, $800.00 in quarters, a ring, I think. I am not sure what all. I do know this, if I would have taken all that, we wouldn't have been without food to feed the kids. There is a lot more to the story but this is the gist of it. There is a lot of bad blood in our family and I was raised by my aunt + uncle and he*

21

had been the Sheriff there years back. The Sheriff that charged me with this was his Deputy and they left on bad terms and I believe he had it out for me. The uncle's house I was charged for breaking into is my mom's brother but is not the uncle that was the Sheriff. Long story! And it's over with now so I am trying to move past all this. I had a lot of anger and resentment for all this because it all started out with trying to feed those babies. But I have sat here for 3yrs and learned to see this as a chance to find out who I really am and who I want to be. I have learned to forgive even when it doesn't seem fair or right. I cannot let my past determine who I am or what my future holds. I have asked for forgiveness from everyone in my life and feel confident I have done my part to move on and leave this behind. I may always have a mark against my name and have to prove that I can be trusted but I am o.k. with that. I know I serve a God that is bigger than all of this and know what He has planned for my life. I know I am an overcomer and if God is for me who can be against me? So, there is another part of my life and another book for you to read. I ask one thing of you and that is to never compare me to what your ex-wife has done to you. I am not here to be her and if that is what you are looking for than you should get with her. I'm not saying this in an ugly way. I am just letting you know how I feel about it. / O.K. I went to church and I feel a lot better but I still don't want to ever be compared to her o.k.? I also need you to know that I don't ever want you to have to worry about me ever taking anything from anyone. I almost got a life sentence behind me trying to do something for someone else. Remember I am not a taker, I am a giver! I have to be honest and tell you I let my feelings get in the way of what you said but it's also something I have to learn to deal with the rest of my life. I am just sorry you had to be the first one to address it. But also thank you that you did because now I know how not to handle it. Sorry if I came off crazy in the first of this part of the letter. We had also talked about what we thought about where this would go and I want you to know I have been praying about this a lot lately. My issue with men is I tend to idolize them and I don't ever in my life want to put anything before God. So, when I feel like I'm putting anything before God I move away a little. But I am not doing that with you. So, at church I get a lady that comes up to me and says that issue you have been worrying and praying about is a blessing from God. So, you do the math and figure it out! So, I am going to go with this and be blessed. You're either going to like me for it or not. But I will be blessed to have just met you and allowed you to be a part of my life. I know you don't take compliments too well but you're a really amazing guy. You are a true blessing and you have blessed me more than you will ever know. I do believe God has His hand in this and no matter what happens it will be from God. I would love to fast forward and see how this turns out but I can't. All I can do is enjoy each moment that is given to me. Well, I have rambled on aimlessly for pages now. So, I am going to put a stamp on this and mail it to you. I really want to throw it away and start over but this has some of my true feelings in it and if I were to rewrite and act like everything was great, I would be lying and I promised not to ever lie. But don't be hurt or *offended! I don't mean it that way at all. But if you do please forgive me! Well, good night and God bless you! Please have sweet dreams and know that you are always in my prayers. Also, there are very few minutes a day that go by that I don't think about you. I always wonder what the next thing you're going to do to make my day. Just know you're very special to me! Let the girls know I think they're beautiful! I can't wait to really meet them and get to know them. You take care of those little Princesses! I can't wait to hear from you very soon!*

Yours Sincerely,
Bonnie

This is out of the "Jesus Calling" I read every day. I hope you enjoy it as much as me. They are letters from Jesus.

My Child,

Taste and see that I am good. This command contains an invitation to experience My living presence. It also contains a promise. The more you experience Me, the more convinced you become of My goodness. This knowledge is essential to your faith-walk. When adversities strike, the human instinct is to doubt My goodness. My ways are mysterious, even to those who know me intimately. As the heavens are higher than the earth, so are my ways and thoughts higher than your ways and thoughts. Do not try to fathom My ways. Instead, spend time enjoying Me and experiencing My goodness.

Psalm 34:8

Isiah 55:8-9   Love, Jesus

I want you to listen to that song "Changed" by Rascal Flatts. That's my life song. I pray that God blesses you greatly this week and you have nothing but praise report to tell me. Also remember that you're always on my mind.

Postmarked on 06 JUL 2015

Coronado, Coronado, Coronado,   *6-29-15*

    With each letter and phone call I began to wonder how can this be? I try to figure out and every time I do it doesn't turn out the way I expected. I give up! Whatever happens, happens. I have always been able to call it for what it is but with you it is a mystery. I know we have talked a lot about the future and I need you to know that I am very excited about you being in my future. There is also a lot of things I would love to say but I can't right now. It has taken me 3 yrs. to learn to deal with my feelings & emotions in here. You know that means holding everything in and learning to work thru things on your own. And now that I have someone that wants me to express them, I kind of don't know how. I have put a block on that but give me some time. I am completely against telling you what you want to hear to make you feel better. I want to say it because I mean it. So, know if I say it, I mean it. I will say this, when I don't talk to you, I feel lost. It seems like I have to rush thru that day to get to the next just so I can hear your voice. I find comfort and peace when I talk to you. Like there is hope for a better future. That maybe I don't have to just settle for anything. I want it to be right though. I don't want to just jump in to this because it sounds wonderful. I want something real and everlasting. I've had all the messed-up relationships I can handle. You're an amazing guy and I can't believe you don't have some wonderful woman in your life already. Someone without a record and a jacked-up past. But you know it makes me sick to my stomach to even think of you not being in my life in some way. What I really need you to know is that I want you to hold off on making any major changes in your life until I see parole. Let's get past this time and then we will see what happens. I'm very excited that you're this involved in my life. But let's get past this parole thing first. I am not going to just disappear out of your life either so stop thinking about that. This is how I see this, if you can be here for me and help support me thru the hard times, then why wouldn't you do it in the good times. It takes a good man to be there for someone in a situation like this. Our families sometimes can't even be there. We sit here and do without a lot of things sometimes because our families forget or they go through hard times too. So, you have been more to me than most have been. I'm really glad we got the phone issue worked out because I don't ever want to be a burden. I want you to do for me because you want to. This is all going to be just fine. I think we just need to go with the flow and see what happens. We don't need to rush anything! Well, of course you know I'm thinking about you, so you can know that you're missed all the time. I got to get in bed so I can go to work. Sleep tight! Sweet dreams!

July 1st!

24

We are now into July! Thank God! I have really been thinking a lot about you here lately! So how has your day been? I hope you felt me thinking about you. I loved the card you sent and the picture. When was it taken? You look like a lawyer I used to know. You really know how to make my day! I was really going thru it yesterday and was really missing you. Never thought I would get a card! Linda loved it and said to tell you we love glitter and could use some more of it sometimes.

She's my little baby sister and easy to entertain. Just give her things that shine and she will be happy for hours! LOL! She's great tho! I haven't gotten your letter yet because I think something is going on in the mail room. We've haven't been getting our mail like we are supposed to. We got some news about the events taking place around the world and it's unbelievable! It makes you think. We need to really get our lives in order! You know it somehow puts an uncertainty on your future. So, if you know that you only had a short time to live, what would you do with the time you had left? And what would you want from others around you and cared about you? (Sorry about my handwriting. My pens only want to work when they want to work.) For me I would want to be out of here for sure and to at least spend some time with my family. Then I would be about my Father's (Heavenly Father) business, and I would just go and take anyone with me that would be willing to go. We live in a world with so many lost people and most of them don't even know they are lost! I have a deep compassion for them and I want to give them the chance to know. I just want to help be a part of the solution and not the problem. But if I had to do it here, I would do it with a smile on my face and peace in my heart. I would also make sure everyone else had that too. We never know when today will be our last! So, what's your input on that? I'm glad God gave me the opportunity to have you in my life. Don't get me wrong if things go down the way they say they will. This will be more of a celebration! That's just what has been running thru my mind. Random thoughts! :p It's been a pretty peaceful day and pretty hot! But what doesn't kill you makes you stronger! Look I got to be strong because I should have been dead many of times! LOL! Well, I'm going to go and pray I get your letter today. Write more later.

July 2nd

All I can say is "This Wonderful Guy". You blow my mind! I'm not real sure what to say! You have me speechless! So... where did you come from? Oh yeah from heaven. It's got to be so. I got all of my mail today and it was a lot. Thank you from the bottom of my heart. You didn't have to do that but I am more than grateful. Words could never express how I feel. You need to hurry and come see me so I can hug you! So, you know everything about me because you sent me a paper that said so. "Sagittarius woman!" You know sometimes I don't mean to be like that but that's who I am no matter how hard I try not to be. So please bear with me. :-) And I will try to be more aware of who you are. Sometimes it's hard for me to talk about feelings and emotions because they have led me down wrong paths in life. But I need you to know I feel them for you. Maybe not as strong as you would like but give me some time. I'm trying to learn to feel the right way. I want you to know that you prove yourself more and more to me every day. To know that you worked extra hours to get me shoes shows me a lot about you. It shows me that if you're willing to take care of me in here I can trust you to do it out there. Why do we have to wait till the 1st of Aug. for you to come? The picture of you and the girls was beautiful! They are true little angels! I can't wait to meet them. We would have so much fun together I promise. I also really felt you in that picture and the coming dawn! I wanted to be there with you so bad. That was amazing! I am glad you let me share that with you. I have got to come spend some time with you when I get out. I know we will have a blast! Really! And stop saying you don't have any one to share it with. You have me to share it with! I think about you just as much as you think about me. Maybe more! O.K. I have a confession to make, when something like this happens in my life I sit around and wait for the moment for something to go wrong and it will be over. So, I'm trying to believe this is real but at the same time wondering when I will mess this up. Now you know a little more about who you are dealing with. Are you sure you're up to the challenge? It's going to take a strong man to deal with me and my issues! I hate that but it's the truth! I wanted to say that I am so glad we got to know each other before you got pictures of me in the world! That is me! Those are some of my favorite pictures! Oh, and the one in prison throw it away! Please! My God I was one messed up ball of emotions. I weighed 167lbs there. I had just gotten to prison and I was in a state of shock. That was me at the lowest of my life. Please don't even show that to anyone. I'm begging you! LOL! Thank you so much for the Birthday Cards. Man, they are perfect. That worked out great. She will love it that you got to sign them. You are the bestest in the world! Hugs & Kisses to you! I'm blowing them so catch them as they come your way. The letter you wrote about sitting in the truck.... I would give anything to be there doing anything with you. You can somehow always make me feel like I'm right there with you! I wanted to jump in that picture with the sunset and just run and give you a big hug. That's how amazing that was. You give me a piece of freedom, a connection with the world. Sometimes I wonder what my hand will look like inside yours! We only have 30 days left to find out! You don't have to worry about losing me. I know that is something that you think about. If worst comes to worse you will always be a close friend! But I do worry about losing you. Because reality is that I'm here and when will something come along in your life that you can really spend time with and you're gone. Just promise me if that happens you will be truthful and let me know. I would rather know than have to sit here wondering. Please don't sugar coat things for me. Just be real and truthful please! Now that I got that out let's move past that. So, by the time you get this letter it will be next week. Mail doesn't run here on holidays and weekends. Hopefully by then you will know the reason I haven't been calling is because the phone is restricted. Something is going on with the bill and you will have *to check on it. I am having Coronado withdrawals! Fix it ASAP! Now I know you have done a lot this week so I will be o.k. with whatever has to happen. You got control over this part. I am really glad, too. I am not good with all this stuff. You have your own business, you know what you're doing. I miss you tho and your voice. It's going to be hard this weekend w/o you but I will be strong. Please send pictures of the fireworks and what you did! I want to be a part of it, too. My little brother's birthday is on the 5th of July. So, this is one of the times of year we all get together! So, don't leave me out! I will be thinking about you and all the kids (yours + mine). Well, have a very blessed night, Sweet dreams, of me! Get some rest and don't work so hard! Oh, I want to try some of that coffee so bad! I love coffee! I also love pedicures and I will hold you to that deal. I want my nails and hair done, too. Will you come sit with me while I get it all done? You very well could be the best thing that has ever happened to me! Time tells all things! Keep me in your prayers as you are always in mine. Wow, check this out. I was praying about this whole thing and look what God gave me. I felt God was saying you needed to hear this, too. We have to know his hand is in this: "Let me show you my way for you this day. I guide you continually, so you can relax and enjoy My Presence in the present. Living well is both a discipline and an art. Concentrate on staying close to Me, the divine Artist. Discipline your thoughts to trust me as I work My ways in your life. Pray about everything; then, leave outcomes up to Me. Do not fear My will, for through it I accomplish what is best for you. Take a deep breath and dive into the depths of absolute trust in Me. Underneath are the everlasting arms!" I thought that was very amazing! Happy 4th of July! I hope you and the girls have a great day! I will be there in Spirit. We will also be having Bar-B-Q here. They are cooking on the grill for us today! It's going to be great! So, I got to talk to you on the phone which was great! We also talked about me being (8 ♥) a charmer. So, what does that mean to you? So, when you do all this research on me and you find out more and more about who you think I am, how do you feel about me? Do you believe it's all true? So, what are you in a deck of cards and what does it mean? I have a hard time believing in some of that stuff because I don't think you can summarize one person and who they are based on their birthday. I am in no way trying to discredit your beliefs in any way. I just can't understand it and maybe you can explain it. I'm sure you don't agree with a lot of my beliefs and I am o.k. with that. I just believe God made us all different and we all have different lives, with different stories, so it's hard for me to believe that you can know someone truly thru just their birth date. So please help me understand! LOL! I think a lot of my misunderstanding of you comes because you touch on little pieces of who you are, here and there. Maybe because you don't want to overwhelm me. Or maybe you are not sure how I will take it. One thing I won't do is judge you for being you! I may not agree or believe the same but it's ok to agree to disagree and be different people. I think you are an amazing guy, just amazing! And take that and believe it. I also believe you have a little bit of a charmer in yourself!*

You know what really is crazy...you have the ability out there to research me to find out who I am. In here I have to go on your word and discernment from God to know who you are. So be real with me please!!! I don't want to get out there and learn something different. That would be heart breaking. I think you are a very nice-looking man with a heart of gold. I thank you for all you do to make my life brighter. I'm very grateful! I do have a very hard time receiving them because then I feel like I owe you something. I am trying not to feel this way but I am not in a position to make promises or repay anything. I just need to say this maybe for myself. Because once again I am a giver and not a taker and I don't have a lot to give to you right now. All I have is myself to give and sometimes that's not much! Well, I'm going to get this ready to mail. You can see I'm more the writer and you're more the talker. I guess that's good because we even things out that way. Except you don't always answer my questions! I'm not trippin' about any of this anymore. One day I will know all I need to know about you. Time tells all things. It's getting closer to the 1st of Aug. and you haven't sent your address on your I.D. remember??! I have to turn that in next Friday! You and the girls have a wonderful day together. Enjoy every moment because they are precious! I would give anything to be with my babies today! Pop some fine works for me! May God bless you each and every day.

Tenderly + Compassionately,

Bonnie

When you worship me in Spirit and truth, you join with choirs of angels who continually praise before my throne. Though you cannot hear their voices, your praise and thanksgiving are distinctly audible in heaven. Your petitions are also heard, but it is your gratitude that clears the way to My Heart. With the way between us wide open, My blessings fall upon you in such abundance. The greatest blessing is nearness to Me – abundant Joy and Peace in My Presence. Practice praising and thanking me continually throughout this day.

John 4:23-24

Psalm 100:4   *Jesus!*

Working the morning shift and with Bonnie on my mind, I felt compelled to ask Pedro to take this photograph of me so that I could send it to her for inspiration.

July 8, 2015

In regard to: Bonnie Wright
DOC#6497319
Crain Unit TC 3-62
1401 State School Road
Gatesville, TX 76599

Honorable Members of the Parole Board

TX Board of Pardons and Parole
3406 South State, Highway 36
Gatesville, TX 76528

Dear Honorable Members of the Parole Board:

My name is Coronado Antonio Borgia, and I am currently a forty-three-year-old full-time employee with the Houston Independent School District, and a volunteer in my community. I am writing on behalf of my friend, Bonnie Ophelia Wright #6497319.

I understand that my friend had made many terrible mistakes that negatively affected the lives of many people and resulted in her being sent to prison. She genuinely understands that as well. She always has a positive attitude when we visit or talk on the phone. She takes full responsibility for the actions that led to her incarceration, and shows considerable remorse. During her time in prison she has taken advantage of many programs that were offered to help her

29

become a better person. She has shown so much positivity in her speech, demeanor and mannerisms, and has also shown tremendous leadership qualities.

If she is granted parole, I am prepared to give her all the support she needs to ensure that she does not return to prison or a negative lifestyle again. That would include financial support, a place to live, and use of a vehicle once she passes her appropriate DPS tests. I will also provide her with emotional support, necessary advice and encouragement; the necessary working tools that she will need to be successful. I will also help Bonnie Wright find employment whereby she can re-enter into the workforce without prejudice of her past.

I believe beyond a doubt that given the opportunity of parole, she will prove to herself and community that she can make considerable contributions to family and society as a whole. Thank you for your time and attention.

Sincerely,
Coronado A. Borgia
Houston, TX 77001

Postmarked on 09 JUL 2015

My Coronado,   *7-8-15*

How have you been these last couple of days? I have been alright! I have not gotten your letter so I am not sure what I am responding to but I have a couple of things on my mind. One, I want to be going on vacation with you, too. I hope y'all have a blast and think of me lots! The other thing is that you want me to draw out what the ranch would look like thru my eyes but look, that's hard for me because it's not mine to do that with. And if it were <u>ours</u> to do that with, I would want your view of things also. I have lived on ranches a lot in my life and love it but I am not sure if I could build my own how I would do it. I just know that horses are my favorite animals and I would have to have some there to ride! I would love to have a house that has that log cabin look on the outside. I don't know! I have tons of ideas but what do you want? Well, we were supposed to go to the store today so that I could blue slip my shoes but we didn't get to go. After we blue slip them we have to wait for the warden to approve them and then I will get them. Hopefully by next week. They are killing me around here! Sorry my pen is acting crazy again. Promise me when I get out, I will always have pens that write and that I will always have a washing machine! Lol! I'm tired of washing by hand. Just more reasons not to ever come back here! It has been a long couple of days around here. It's like the days are creeping by. I'm going to go *and wait on mail hoping to get your letter. I will call you later, also. I just wanted you to know I was thinking about you and was missing you. Write more later!*

So here I am! I got both your letter and talked to you. You know I have been doing a lot of thinking about the future and this is what I have come up with. There is no doubt that I need to go to my mother's when I get out. Just hear me out on this please. There are some things I need to take care of there. I am not saying that you can't be in my life at this point. My family needs to see the change in me. They need to know this is real, too. I have also been a missing piece of their lives for years now and they are just as excited as you are. Will they accept? There's no doubt in my mind! You might become more welcome than me! I have picked men and put myself first in a lot of areas of my life when it has come to my kids that I believe I owe them a little bit of mommy time alone for a while. Not that I wouldn't introduce you! Look I would love to promise you all the things that sound so great <u>but</u> then reality hits me and I know I have to be there for my family, <u>also</u>. So, if you care about me as much as you think you do than you will allow me this time to get everything right. My kids are my world and I have missed out on so much of their lives already I just want to be the mom they need for a minute. I also realize they have lives they are comfortable in and may want to go back to those lives. And I have to be o.k. with that but there is also the chance they will want to stay with me after a while. Then what would you think about that? I have 4 boys and they are all momma's boys! I know my kids and I am sure they will end up with me sooner than I may be ready for them to. I will never turn them away. Also, my oldest son will be coming out of prison about the same time as me and I can't just leave him out there. I can't save him but I can be there as his mother. He has not had much support from anyone thru this whole ordeal and I need to be there for him. My daughter, well, let's just say this could go two ways. She could end up next to me and never want to leave or she could be in a point in her life where she is comfortable and just needs me to be mother for a while. So that's some food for thought!! I come with a package that not too many people can deal with. I know I told you I would send you pictures but it's hard looking thru them and it's hard to part with them, even for a couple of days. Let me tell you these are some amazing kids and they have supported me thru all of this. It hasn't always been easy but they have always been here for me. As for people that know I wrote my oldest two about you but really no response yet. I told my best friend from the world about you and she said as soon as she gets the money to get ink for her printer, she will send me pictures to send to you. She was my sister-in-law at one time. She was married to my baby brother Derrick. Her name is Bridget. I'm sure Casey's grandma knows because I'm sure she read her letter and now the whole family may know about you! LOL! Oh, yeah, you may be more famous in my family then I even know. I forgot about her knowing! Don't worry it won't take long and I will be hearing about you. News spreads fast in my family! And extended family! And you don't have to worry about Linda me giving any more men. She knows *you have me busy enough. I really do like you and they know that. They also see how happy I am, so they are happy with me. I have one friend Beth that is very dear to me and we have also done all of our time together. We three have done it all together. So, this is her deal, I think she's a little jealous or just really lonely. So sometimes she's not so happy for me. So, if you have buddies that need a pen-pal I have one for them. She's only got her adopted grandma here for her. She's had a hard life but she is an amazing person! I just hate it that she's so lonely, sometimes. She also doesn't want me to be hurt anymore. So, help me give her something to do! PLEASE! So, I am not sure how I am going to handle myself at this visit so bear with me. I've checked it out and we should have a pretty good officer those days. I am so glad you are coming sooner.*

I want to see you so bad. I think we will know a lot more about how we feel after this! You will have no worries about other men in my life. You're it! My Coronado! I just pray God makes this all right because I don't want any one hurt! You're an amazing guy and you deserve a life time of happiness. You have so much going on for you and sometimes I believe you are too good to be true. The last thing I would ever want to do is hurt you. Look I would jump into this head first and worry about things later. Go all out but that's not always good. I'm here for not thinking things thru. I may seem colder than you would like but I have to keep myself in check. I have more feelings than you think! I just have to give it time to make sure they are real or if they are just because that's what we want it to be. We may meet each other and just know we will always be friends and it could go just the way we hope it will. I need you to know I pray every night that God will not allow this to go anywhere it doesn't need to go. I don't want this blessing to turn into a mess because I'm like Nike and "just do it". I really care about you and I'm very happy I have you in my life. Thank you for dealing with me! Most of all thank you for just being you, "My Coronado". Thank you for being more than I ever dreamed of. You are so gentle with me and you let me be me, even when I'm trippin'! You make me miss you even before we say goodbye or even hang up the phone. I just want to be out of here so I can talk to you as long as I want to, when I want to. Thanks for writing me a Support Letter and being a part of my parole process. I miss you real Big! You're in all my thoughts and some of my dreams. It's been a very long week and I've been very home sick so keep me in your prayers. Well, my dear, I have to get up at like 3:45 in the morning so I'm going to end this and get to bed. It's 10:15! I need my beauty sleep! You have a wonderful rest of the week and I will talk to you on Friday. Oh, I love the middle name! Really! We won't get into that right now. That's a line I won't cross at this point! Oh, and you better not be out drinking the family money up at the bars! What!?! I know who hangs out at bars and it better not be you! You want to see me trip...then go hang out at the bar! LOL! Now you go and enjoy life till I get out of here and then we will see what changes. By the way I'm not a drinker at all. It's just never been my thing! But with all this said have a great night! I will be thinking about you. I miss you lots! Lots! Also, always let the girls know I say hello. I am very happy they are happy about me. I'm very happy that I make you happy! Tons of hugs + kisses your way! Good night!

Completely Amazed,

Bonnie

P.S.

I can't wait to really learn who you are on the 25th! You leave me hanging on so much! I don't really wonder. I'm sending pics of the kids! Please send them back soon! I really trip about these but I really trust you! (It's like letting them stay for the weekend without me!)

Postmarked on 20 JUL 2015

I received a "Thinking of you..." card printed at the *Hobby Print Shop* in Marlin, Texas.

My Coronado,   *7-17-15*

I just wanted to let you know that I was thinking about you and that I really have missed you. I know you're having a wonderful time with your family and I'm very happy for you. Have a Blast, Babe! It makes me happy to know you are happy. You have been such a blessing to me and I also want to be one for you. You truly are amazing and I don't ever want to not have you in my life! I know that we only have 8 days till we get to see each other eye to eye! I can't wait. It's going to be great! Thank you for all you do and just for being you. You don't know how much that means to me! You're the greatest in my book, Tons of hugs and kisses your way. Tell the girls I said hi and I hope they had a blast! I want to see pictures!

.. and the many

Blessings you bring

Into my life.

You make me miss you more and more each day! It's almost hard to believe it's all even real! I can't wait to see you! Hurry and get yourself over here!

Bonnie!

Postmarked on 20 JUL 2015

GATESVILLE INSTITUTIONAL PAROLE OFFICE

3406 SOUTH STATE HWY 36

GATESVILLE, TEXAS 76528

STATE OF TEXAS

BOARD OF PARDONS AND PAROLES

July 15, 2015

Mr. Coronado Borgia

Re: Wright, Bonnie TDCJ-CID #6497319

Dear Mr. Borgia:

This is to acknowledge receipt of your correspondence dated July 08, 2015.

The information you provided will be placed in the offender's permanent parole file to be available for consideration by the parole panel at the appropriate time.

Respectfully,

D.J. / C.G.

IPO II / Assistant Regional Supervisor

Cc: File

My Coronado,

I'm writing you this letter because you are all I can seem to think about. I know that you are coming in a couple of days and I'm a nervous wreck! LOL! Not because I don't know, but because of how things will be after we see and touch each other for the first time. You are something more than I have ever dreamed of and that scares me. It's like you can read my mind sometimes and you always know what to do to make me smile. I never have to ask you for anything because you listen so well. You always pay attention to details and that is so wonderful. You better watch out I could get used to that. You talk about spoiled! No, for real, you make me feel really special! You make me feel good about myself and you give me a reason to keep going. I also want to do the same for you but what I can do is very limited. I wish I could do more because I would. I do want to spend some time with you when I get out. I don't want me going home to push you away. I need you to support me thru this and really be there for me. You are the only one who knows the new me, besides Beth and Linda, that I will have contact with, out there. Look I'm really going to need you out there. My family loves me and they want to help me but they can also overwhelm me.

I don't know what is going to happen from here on out but I need you to know you have shown me how to live again. To find hope that things can be more that what they have always been. That I can do anything I want to do or go anywhere I want to go. I have a hard time with trusting anyone including myself but you have given me no reason not to trust you. And believe me I have done things just to see if I could trust you. You have always come thru and that's a <u>Big</u> thing for me. The only thing that bothers me is you don't talk about your past and when I bring it up you try to go around it. I don't really push the issue because you never know what someone else has been thru and how it may be hard to talk about. But I'm interested and would never judge you. I don't know I'm just very open about everything in my life and I guess I think everyone else should be also. But I know that is not the case. I just want to know everything about you. Not only the good but the bad, too. Those are the things that mold us into who we are today. You may not be comfortable and if that is so, what can I do to make you more comfortable with me? I just want to be here for you like you are for me. I don't talk about my past to you because I'm not sure you can handle it or would want to even know. I will openly tell you anything you would like to know. I will tell you this it's not all good. My mom has always told me that God must have something so huge planned for me because if someone has happened to them, it has been me. I will say this, God has had his hands on me the whole time because I have come out with a great report and smelling like roses. I'm not bragging one bit, I'm *just telling you how great my God has been, I know you may have lots of questions you're afraid to ask but really, I'm pretty sure I can handle it. My kids are a touchy subject but I can get thru it pretty well. Oh yeah, I need you to know that my criminal history is all within the 3yrs I was on drugs. The one where I was 31yrs old was because the two youngest one's dad had come in drunk one night, like always, and started hitting on me. I never knew what he was going to do. Crazy life. Anyways, this night I was tired of him waking me up hitting on me. So, I grabbed a knife and told him to get out of the house. He did and then he came running at me and grabbing for the knife. So, I dropped it and he tried to catch it with his hand and it cut him. The next day he went to the cops to tell them I had took his money which he had spent it that night out partying and they asked what happened to his hand and he told them I cut him. He just forgot to tell him he beat my head on the concrete for 15mins before he left. I had to go stay with my mom and brother so they could help me watch the kids. While they were at work the cops came and arrested me. He got the kids and that night he was arrested on a warrant. They almost had to rush me to the ER from the jail because of dizziness and major headaches. My stepdad bonded me out the next day. He bonded him out that same night within minutes. I had a restraining order where I could go around him and the kids but within a couple of hours of me being out, he went to the court house and dropped the charges. I stayed with my mom and brother for a while but of course I went back because, one, I was stupid to think he would change and two, the kids wanted to be at their home. I know I didn't have to explain this to you but I wanted to. I need you to know I have nothing to hide. Nothing! I have been arrested 3 times for possession of a controlled substance. My first one was dropped to a lower charge and I got probation that I completed early. The other two were dismissed. My house was raided because of some mess my son had gotten into. I went to jail for my third possession but it was dropped because the sheriff didn't have a search warrant at the time he came into my house. Then you know all about this charge. That is my criminal history. I had a few warrants for my arrest for traffic tickets but I think my brother has paid most of them off for me to make sure I have a clean record when I get out. Other than that, I'm a pretty good girl. I bet you're thinking "Oh my goodness. What have I gotten myself into?" You will see Sat. that my heart is pure and I'm a very sincere person. I have a huge heart and I'm really a good girl! I can't wait to see you. I pray I meet all your expectations. I have already written more than I planned but I guess you needed to hear this or I just needed to say it. I feel like if it's out in the open, then you will feel better asking questions if you need to. I also love the idea that you want to have a project for us to do together! I would enjoy it so much to help you plan out your ranch. Before I got on drugs and got with this last man that most call my husband, I wanted a divorce more than you could ever know. I just feel like that would put so much closure to my past! Random thought! Anyways, I lived on a ranch trained cutting horses. My kids were involved and everything. So, when I think of a ranch, I would set it up like that but I know that is not what this ranch you have would be used for. I love horses! We got to have horses. I love to ride! Other than that, I'm really not picky. Just peace and quiet! A place to relax and enjoy life. Somewhere I could fall asleep on your chest and drool all over you! That is my favorite place to sleep is on someone's, I care about, chest. I usually get woke up with spit all over them! LOL! How would you like that? Tell me now if that will be a problem! LOL! I think that's really cute but you may not. Oh, here's another big thing about me. When I'm with someone you better let the whole world know we are together when we are in public! You better hold my hand or something. I just think that's so cute and I like to see people holding hands. You better act like you enjoy being with me. I will make an announcement to let everyone know. I will embarrass you until you do! LOL! O.K. I think I've said enough and it's late, late, late at night. I can't see what I'm writing and I'm sure every other word is misspelled. But you will understand, I hope! I just wanted you to have something great to read when you got home from our visit! My life is so wonderful and that's because you are in it. I wake up most mornings wondering how this happened but I think God did it. I can't wait to talk to you tomorrow! One phone call then our visit. I want you to know these phone calls get harder and harder because I never want them to end. And on the days I don't call, OMG, they take forever! One day soon I will be out of here and we won't have to worry about this anymore. I'm going to end this now. Baby, have a wonderful evening! Keep a smile on your face because you keep one on mine. You are the best. Go to bed tonight knowing that I need you in my life! Keep me in your prayers as you are always in mine.*

With all my heart,

Bonnie

I miss you really bad today! I only wonder what you are doing. I wish you here with me. NO, NO, LOL! I was there with you! Sweet dreams, Sweetheart!

Postmarked on 30 JUL 2015

I received a hand-made colorful card from her, or by another inmate on her behalf: I had received my Associate's Degree in May (weeks before we knew each other). There was no ceremony, no cake and no party. All of that wasn't necessary to feel that I had accomplished a milestone in my life, and Bonnie acknowledged and made me feel special with a personalized and thoughtful card. Ah, the simple things!

Within the very thoughtful card was a letter and inside that letter, another. It read:

My Coronado, 7-28-15

To the Sweetest Man I know! How has your day been? I pray it has been wonderful because you deserve nothing less. I wanted to write you to congratulate you on your Degree in Arts! I need you to know that I understand how big of an accomplishment that is. I know over the phone it may not seem that I am as excited but I need you to know that I am overwhelmed with excitement for you. You have achieved what I have been trying to achieve for years now. There is not a whole lot I can do from where I am but I wanted to make it a little special so I am sending you a card to help you remember this day. You are very special to me and I thank you dearly for allowing me to be a part of this special day with you and most of all to be in your life. I know we let time limit us and I know we may not have known each other for long but I cannot imagine my life without you in it. You have made a huge impact on my life and in such a way that I view life differently now. You have shown me how to have true faith and totally rely on the Lord for all things. You have also allowed me to be just me and you accept me just as I am. You have taught me how to dream big and never limit yourself or God. So, when I say you are amazing it is because you are just that! So, smile because you have accomplished so much not only in your life but also in mine. You are proof to me that dreams and possibilities are endless when you believe in yourself! So, Babe, please know that I am celebrating this day with you. Tons of Hugs and Kisses your way. I would have loved to have been there to share this moment with you in person! You are truly the best! I can't seem to find the words to let you know how much you mean to me but I will say you will <u>always</u> have a special place in my heart and it grows larger and larger each day. Have a great day and rest of the week. Thank you for all that you do to make me happy but all you really need to do is just be you! Take some time off from your business and school to get some rest. You really need it, Babe! You haven't been yourself lately because you're really distracted by all that's going on. You know Rome wasn't built in a day! I miss my baby really bad but I also understand and support you! My prayers are with you and you are in my thoughts often. Have a great day and Congratulations, Baby!

Yours truly,

Bonnie

Philippians 4:13

Psalm 1:3

Proverbs 3:6

The smaller note read as such:

Sweetie,

Hey I need to ask you to please feel free to write my son if would like to. He is a great kid but has never had a father in his life. I think it would do him some good. I think you would be a good example for him. He's a lot like his mother! He doesn't get much mail and he doesn't have a lot of support out there. Just handle him with care. That is still my Baby Boy! I just wanted you to have my approval to write him if that's what you wish to do. I want you to know you're great! Have a great day!

Hugs + Kisses,

Bonnie

Let the girls know I said hi and I think they have an awesome Dad! I will get to meet them before you get this! Yeah! I can't wait!

Postmarked on 04 AUG 2015

Happy Anniversary

God fills life with Love and Laughter on the way to...

Happily Ever after.

Because of my scheduling and visitation rights with my daughters every other weekend, I thought it beneficial to take Veronica and Julianna with me on a road trip to Central Texas, not only to spend quality time together but I also wanted to show them that there were no limitations or boundaries on helping those in need. Giving them this introduction to philanthropy and social science was also my way of showing them that not only were there consequences to actions, but there was hope through compassion and humanity. Granted, they were only nine and ten years of age, and it would be a short visit at the correctional facility but when the alarm rang at five in the morning, we all got up and got ready for another fun-filled adventure with Dad.

It was roughly a three and half-hour drive from my apartment in Houston to Gatesville and it was my second time venturing out so I packed a small cooler with sandwiches, snacks and water. The girls brought their pillows so they could relax in the backseat. In order to utilize the day we needed to leave no later than five-thirty so we could make the early roll-call and be there in time when they open their doors for visitors. After filling the gas tank and cleaning the windshield, we were on our way towards I-45 headed northbound.

When we reached Huntsville an hour later, we all waved at the Sam Houston Statue and I then realized that we were a third of the way there. Traffic was less congested as we were leaving the city and suburban neighborhoods and entering pure highway lanes full of courteous truck drivers and other vehicles. It wouldn't be long until we would approach rural farmlands on each side before our first pit stop in Madisonville.

"Thank you, Lord. I am so happy to be driving through God's country. This is so beautiful." I marveled in complete bliss with the sense the I was free to see and experience the wonders before me. The fields of grass, the grazing cows, the remnants of old barns, and looking in the rearview mirror – my daughters peacefully sleeping on their soft pillows, and everything started to illuminate as the sun was slowly rising and reminding me that it was the beginning of a new dawn.

This wasn't our first time visiting Buc-cees, as we would stop there for beef jerky, sometimes ice, but always to use their super-clean restroom facilities on our way to San Antonio but it would be their first time visiting the one in Madisonville.

"Hey, girls, we're making our first pit stop. We're almost half-way there already."

"Cool, dad." Veronica said as she yawned and rubbed her eyes from her slumbering. Julianna quietly got out and closed the door behind her then walking closely with us. They were having a good time. I knew it to be true since no one was bickering or complaining about anything because they were with me and everything was a subtle learning moment. I think they were just tired.

When we left I turned on some Country music, not too loud, but enough for me to get into a good 'ole country livin' mood, filled with appreciation, life and maybe some twang. From I-45 I took Route 7 West and passed by more farms, and small towns until we reached the town of Marlin, where we stopped to have breakfast at the McDonald's, and afterwards at the Shell station to fill'er up, but also to collect as many quarters as I could, no more than twenty-dollars in total, since all the vending machines at the prison only took quarters.

When we reached the correctional facility entrance by nine, we had to exit the vehicle while they searched under the hood, the trunk and the inside of my Hyundai, I guess in search for weapons or other passengers. After that checkpoint, we drove another mile towards the next checkpoint where we had to park and check in with the Correction Officers at the door. I gave them Bonnie's information and they verified that I was on her approved list of visitors. The girls also went through the process, but they were experts at it from all the times we travelled at the airports and had to go through their security checkpoints. The girls were never in any danger, as I would never allow that to happen. Like meeting anyone new, they were quiet.

Postmarked on 04 AUG 2015

Hey Sweetheart, 8-2-15

It was amazing to meet your beautiful little girls. I know that me and those girls could have a blast together. You have done a great job raising them. They are some very well-mannered girls. I also love the connection y'all have with one another. I can tell they love their Daddy and their Daddy loves them. I know the girls were very quiet because they didn't know me but I must warn you that I'm not sure my kids will be the same. They are like their momma and don't know a stranger! It was a wonderful visit and I always hate to see you leave. I really, really do. And plus, they always have to be in a hurry to get us out of there. I do want to tell you that it means the world to me that you care about me enough to want me to meet your girls. That speaks volumes to me. You have a wonderful little family and I am honored that you would want me to be a part of it. I wish that you could meet mine and I pray you will very soon. You can see thru how my brother has been that they are very friendly people. They are very accepting of others and love to meet new people. They are a little loud and there are lots of them (my family). The only one of my children you could get to know right now is my oldest, Raul. He's a really great kid but he's also not afraid to speak what's on his mind. He's a really awesome person. He has always been with me and followed my lead, but I haven't always been the best leader. I can say that he has forgiven me and we have learned some big lessons thru all of this. You will have to wait till I get home to meet the others. Sorry! :p I really love it that we are at a place that we are comfortable with each other. You know it seems so unreal at times. I wonder how did this all happen to me and so fast! I know that you have really spoiled me and I can be a brat when I call and you're busy living life! LOL! I'm going to work on that because I know it's not all about me! I know you got a lot to accomplish before Sept. but I also want you to see you are stretching yourself thin. I don't like to see you like that. I support you all the way in all you do but not when I see you worn out. In the end is it all that important? I'm not sure how you feel about that but it feels like you're doing too much. Maybe I feel like that because I want more time for me! I just see it this way, all these earthly achievements are not getting us anywhere in Heaven. I am not saying don't try to strive to be someone here on earth but you don't have to kill yourself trying to get there, Babe. I'm just really concerned about you that's all. On a better note Thank you so much for staying contact with my family and sending them a picture of us. That means a great deal to me. Also thank you so much for taking time out of your life to be a part of mine. I can't express or find the words to say how grateful I am for you.

So, what do you think about all this? Do you think I can be all you are looking for? So, what's going on with your job change? See you have so much going on, Babe. I don't want you getting a job so far away I can't get to you when I get out. Or to where you can't see me every once in a while! I know you have to do what you have to do but man I'm getting so used to having you in my life. I don't want you to be taken out of it. I don't know just keep me updated on that. It's going to be a long few days not hearing your voice but I wanted to give you time to get things done and also get some <u>rest</u>! I will miss you more than you will ever believe but absence makes the heart grow fonder! You will miss me, I know, but it will be easier on you! Oh, I have to say you are not as shy as you put on. I like it that you are not afraid to make a risky move! You don't know how great it felt to have someone to touch or grab your butt after this long locked up. I feel like a caged animal and when they let me out, you might want to be rested up! When I hold your hands, I wonder how they will feel when you can really hold me or touch me. You know sometimes I feel like you're more than you say you are. Maybe because you are afraid to express yourself for fear of how I will take it or react. But if you haven't noticed by now it's hard to even get me to blush! I don't want this to turn into something crazy either but I want you to let your guard down a little! I hope you have received your other mail I sent. I just wanted to celebrate a little with you. I'm really proud of you! Well, I'm going to get this in the mail. Please let the girls know I am very happy I got to meet them and they can come back anytime they want. But only if they want! They are some amazing girls and I can't get out and spend some time with them. With you too, Babe! I will be praying really hard for you to get everything done that needs to be done and that all your plans will come thru just how you want them to. I also pray you will have peace and rest thru it all.

Sincerely,

Bonnie

Kisses just for you, Babe!

Just a reminder of how it feels to have your lips on mine!

Linda wanted me to tell you that if you ever see my boobs you won't be a butt man no more!

Postmarked on 11 AUG 2015

GIC

Always be proud of your achievements, and use them to fulfill your dreams.

You have so much going on and I am very glad you have allowed me to be a part of it all. I have worked very hard these last few weeks and it has paid off greatly. Just wanted you to know how proud of you I am. Wish I could be there!

Sincerely,

Bonnie

Now maybe you can relax! Maybe some extra time for me! xoxoxo

My Sweetheart, 8-12-15

I hope this letter reaches you with all the joy I sent with it. You know the last couple of months have been amazing and have been more than I could have ever hoped for. But these last couple of weeks have been almost overwhelming. We have had so much going on in our lives that it's almost unbelievable. We have been blessed beyond measures. So, I have been thinking that if life can be this great from in here how much more will it be out there. I know that I haven't expressed my feelings a lot to you but that's only because of fear of being hurt. I want you to know that you have turned this worse nightmare into something beyond words for me. I never knew that someone could make someone so happy. You do that for me! This also is very terrifying to know that I could lose it. Not because I think that will happen but you know when you really care about someone you always wonder if they feel the same way. I have a hard time expressing myself because there are just some words that are very abused and misused and I am careful not to use them in that way. But I care about you more than you know.

So, I have finally seen parole! I believe you spoke that into happening. I have learned one thing about you, you do not like to wait! LOL! You want to make things happen and this is one thing that is out of our control. So, we have to wait. Me on the other hand have learned how to wait with the best of them. That's all you do here is wait! You wait for them to call you for work, then you wait for them to sign you out, then you wait for chow, then for a shower. You wait to see parole, then you wait for an answer, then you wait for an exit lab pass, then you wait on a releasing pass. Wait. Wait. Wait! You also learn you have no control over things. You lose all control when you walk in these gates. But I do love that about you. You make things happen! So, you have passed your first test and on to your next one. I'm very Happy and Proud of you! Man, I wish I could be there to really experience the full effect of it. If life is this much fun and exciting with you, I don't ever want to be away from you! I can't wait to see you this weekend. You don't know how much I missed you last weekend. Everyone was asking how my visit went and was surprised you didn't come. I just told them you had business to take care of. Oh, I also wanted you to know that I'm sorry if I was short and things on the phone yesterday. I was so tired! That's no excuse. I know and I'm very sorry! You know that parole stuff will take everything out of you. I'm better though I slept so hard last night and I had good dreams of you! Well, Babe, I just wanted to let you know I was thinking about you. You know it's like the more mail I send you the less I get! Hmmm! I'm just trying to say mail call around here really sucks! Hint! Hint! I understand you have a lot on your mind but it better not be taking

46

the place of me! LOL! Well, I'm going to go eat something and maybe take a nap. It is really cool here today. It may even rain! Good time to sleep! I really miss you, Babe!

So, I went to eat and it was very good! I can't sleep so I sit down and thought I would make the girls something so they could get something in the mail also. It's not much but it's the thought that counts. I make little stuff like this for my bunch all the time. I'm sure by now you can tell I don't make all the cards I send you. But now you will know the one I did make. I like lots of color! Bright colors! Happy colors, so that when people open them up it puts a smile on their face. I just wanted the girls to know they are special too.

I have been really bored all day. We have had one of the worst officers, so I have had to just sit in the dorm. I've kept my mind busy thinking about you. I wonder what you think about things because you never reply to anything I write you. I wonder what goes thru your mind! I have a hard time writing anymore because I feel like it's a one-sided conversation! What's going on? You make me crazy sometimes! LOL! I wrote my mom and sent my brother (Luke) a birthday card. His birthday is on the 16th. I just wrote to tell my mom about my interview with parole. I sent all the kid's pictures of us and wrote and told them about you. I also wrote Raul and talked to him a lot about you. So, I should get lots of mail real soon!!! You know I don't hear much from the kids until they know I have someone in my life then they want to get in my business. It's o.k. though. I can tell my mom and my brother are ok with me and you because I haven't heard anything about it. I guess Luke approved of you or he would have said something for sure. I will let you know what everyone says if they say anything at all. I know they are just glad that I took 3 years to find myself before I started talking to someone again. Hey, I need you to let me know when the girls' birthdays are. I know Veronica is in Feb. but I don't remember the day. I would hate to miss one of their birthdays.

O.K. now that's enough of random thoughts! What's my amazing Baby been up to today? I can't wait for the day when I get out of here and spend some time with you. Just to see what your days are really like. To get to know you in every different situation and to see how you really handle things. I know there are so many things I don't know about you. But look, Buddy, when I'm in your face and there is no one around to control the situation, then what? I know it won't be too much longer. Maybe even sooner than you can believe. But for now, I can't wait to see you this weekend. I love to feel you touching me and your lips on mine. They just don't give us enough time. One more reason never to come back here again. I have tons of reasons never to come back here but you know if I would have never come here, I would have never met you. So, I thank God for turning this into something so great! Well, I'm going to finish this and get this in the mail. I believe that one of these days you're going to sit down and really tell me how you feel. I know you're not shy at all. So, what is it? Well, until then know that feelings for you are greater than I can find words right now to say. You are always in my thoughts and prayers. I hope next week is even more exciting than this week! Millions of Hugs and Kisses coming your way!

Truly yours,

Bonnie

P.S.

If I gave you the key to my heart what would you do with it???

My Child,

My Peace is the treasure of treasures: the pearl of great price. It is an exquisitely costly gift, both for the Giver and the receiver. I purchased this peace for you with My blood. You receive this gift by trusting me in the midst of life's storms. If you have the world's peace – everything going your way – you don't seek My unfathomable Peace. Thank Me when things do not go your way, because Spiritual blessings come wrapped in trials. Adverse circumstances are normal in a fallen world. Expect them each day. Rejoice in the face of hardship, for I have overcome the world.

Love,

Jesus

Matthew 13:46

James 1:2

John 16:33

You know this little letter from Jesus has helped me thru the most of these 3 years. You know he really knows what he is talking about. When you are in a trial you can look behind and see you just came thru a victory and look at the end and see you are about to come to another victory. If you've never been in prison you don't know how to be free. If you haven't ever been hurt you don't know how to heal. If you never have hated someone you would never know how to love. You see how all blessings come with a trial.

Have a Blessed Day, Babe!   *Xoxoxo*

Hey Girls,   *8-12-15*

    I just wanted to write and let you know that it was amazing to meet you both. Think you are two beautiful little girls. You both have sweet little spirits and very quiet voices. I know that meeting me for the first time was a little uncomfortable but I would love to get to know you both a lot more. I think you have the best Daddy in the world and I care about him a lot. So that means I care about you two also. I know that sometimes it might feel weird when you are around me but it will get easier the more I am in your life. I want you to know that any time you would like to come with your Dad to visit, I would love to have you here. I sat down the other day and was drawing some little things for my kids and I couldn't leave you guys out. I think everyone needs to know they are special and you both are special to me. I know it's not much but I hope it puts a smile on your face. I also wanted y'all to have mail also. It feels good to know someone is thinking about you. Plus, it's not fair that your Daddy gets all the mail. Well, I'm going to get this in the mail so you can get it by this weekend. I hope to see you this weekend at visitation but if not, I will see you another time! Have a great Day! Smile because you are both very special!

Sincerely,

Bonnie

My Baby,   *8-17-15*

   How are you doing? You know that I am great as long as you are in my life. I think we had a very good visit this weekend! Thank you for being consistent in my life. You know I have not had a lot of that. Also thank you for being patient with me. You are just too good to be true sometimes and that scares me. My feelings for you go way beyond like. I know how I feel but I would never say those words in a letter. You amaze me with all you do and I could see you in my life. In fact, I think you may be just what I need in my life. My reason for writing is to congratulate you on the completion of your degree. I do believe it is final now! So, me and the girls got together to let you know that we are celebrating this with you. We are having a party for you all the way over here. Maybe the next celebration we will all be out there! Linda & Beth love you to death. They think you and the girls are wonderful for me. They already had us married and the whole wedding planned out before I got in! LOL! They had a lot to say about you! All good!

   I want you to know that everything I have said has been true. I have really fallen for you and I'm scared of being hurt. Believe me I'm really trying here and you have the whole place full of fans rooting you on! I haven't gotten your letter yet but I can't wait to see what it says! I will tell you the real truth here; I'm really holding back right now to see what happens. To see what happens with you and parole. I want you to know that kids are my weakness and I love those little girls. I think they are precious and the sweetest tings ever. Oh, also Veronica and my baby John have the same birthday! They are also the same age! I thought that was really cool! Please let the girls know that I loved spending time with them. We had a lot of fun even if we didn't have any quarters! LOL! I told my friend Miranda that sat next to us she said she wished she would have heard me because she would have given the girls some. I do know I had fun. Oh, and also, I know I need to chill on the phone. I'm going to stop calling so much! I miss you real really bad when I don't get to hear your voice but I'll stop being a brat! LOL! I understand now that the phone has been restricted for a couple of days. I miss you really bad but I know I need to chill. Just know that I miss you and I'm thinking about you! Let me know if I get an answer anytime soon? I loved the card you sent me and the one you sent for Beth. You're really amazing! Congrats on your _Big_ Achievement! Keep me in your prayers as you are always in mine! Sweet Dreams! Tons of Hugs + Kisses!

Missing you Real Bad!

Bonnie

P.S.

I'm a little worried because I haven't heard from you since y'all left here. Just like to know y'all made it home o.k.   *xoxoxo*

Chapter 3:

Parole

Postmarked on 24 AUG 2015

Sit down because we need to talk! I do love you, I just need to vent! xoxoxo

My Coronado,   8-23-15

   I hope this letter finds you doing better than our last phone call. I do understand this was hard on you and I'm sorry. But I never saw it coming myself. So, I have to let you know that this was a very hard blow for me. My ship got hit and sank! This is probably one of the hardest times I've had since being locked up. You know I sit here for 3 years doing everything humanely possible to make sure everything would be right when I saw them and knowing in my heart there was nothing in my way of going home. Then they tell me I have to stay here for another year. I don't think or know if you understand that they just took another year of my life away. My children will be another year older and God only knows how much more of their lives I will miss. Not including everything in my family's lives. Then there is your life and the girls. I lost all hope and my life was shattered! So, what do I do? I call you in my worst desperate time of need and I'm left there feeling worse than I came. You said some things that were discouraging and completely out of line. I know that you may think this is harsh, what I'm saying, but it's how I feel. I've also had a couple of days to get out of my feelings. First of all, you never discourage someone in prison by ever making a comment about them ever having to do more time. You made a remark about what happens when I don't make parole next year or the next year and 18 years from now. You spoke that into my life and now the thoughts are free to run wild. You know I called you to get encouragement. To hear someone tell me it's going to be ok. Not to talk about how depressed they were and how they needed to go on vacation. You know it was like this heavy burden on you and you needed to get away. You said you were the same guy but I'm not sure I know this person. I understand it hurt you but your words were sharp and cut deep. I got off the phone and cried harder than I had. I'm not saying this to hurt you but I need you to understand how much it hurt me. You know I told you to really think about this and let me know if you think you can still do this. I need you to really think this over and I will understand if you cannot but if you choose to, I need someone to encourage me and build me up and not bring me down. Look I really needed someone right now and I know it's not your responsibility to be here for me but you have been here all the rest of the time I just thought you would be.

I just felt that you were here thru all the good times but when the heat got turned up you backed up. You know I don't know if you know this but out of all the times I could have used a visit, it would have been this weekend. I know you had other plans and that's great. I hope everything turned out better than what you wanted. I wasn't even going to write this letter but I felt if I didn't you would never know my feelings. I would also only be hurting myself by holding it in and letting it turn into bitterness. Then when the next thing that rubbed me wrong, I would let it all out in an ugly way. That is the old Bonnie and I chose to do things different. I also chose to act differently. I want you to know that me not calling you doesn't all have to do with being upset with you but it has to do with you being busy this weekend and I needed time to get myself together. I needed to pick up the pieces and try to just feel again. I have been numb for a couple of days now but now I can see the sunshine shining thru the clouds. I can hold my head up and walk on. I know I am stronger than that and it's going to take a lot more than this mess to get me down. I know that God turns messes into miracles every day. I thank you for all you have done, doing and going to do in my life. You have been amazing and this can be one of those things we get thru or not. You have control of your life and what you want to do with it. I have limited options and only can do what they allow me to do. So, what I'm saying is that my feelings for you haven't changed and I already forgive you for it all. I just want you to be aware of what I need and don't need in my life. I get enough negative here. I need a little more positive! I did get to talk to my family and we all cried for the whole 20 minutes. They are getting the phone on and they will be here to see me in the next 60 days. So, I asked them to please let me know so that y'all would not come at the same time. Raul hasn't gotten his answer yet but we are hoping for the best. My youngest 3 got to see each other and spend a couple of days together after being apart for over 3 years. So that was a blessing for me! They all got pictures for me and they are sending them in. I just feel so much better knowing they are going to be o.k. Really, I just needed my momma! Days are still a little hard but I'm getting back into the groove of things. Today I played Jesus in a play we did for church. That was really stepping out there. But I figure why not get out of my comfort zone now that I am not comfortable of a place in my life. They want to make me leader over the choir now but I'm not sure I want all that responsibility right now. Linda and Beth still haven't gotten an answer yet but I'm sure they will be out of here soon! They are going thru it tho. You know the wait is what almost kills you. I haven't really heard from any of my kids yet but I'm sure I will in a couple of weeks. I have to give them some time to get over all the hurt, too. I haven't told Raul yet because I don't want him to get discouraged waiting on his answer. All I know is this. I have made it thru 3 years. I can do another one. I know how to act and what I need to do to make my time go fast. So, what do you think on your end? Has your view on this whole thing changed? All I ask is to be real with me. I'm going to get this in the mail so that you know that I still love you and I'm thinking about you. No matter what happens along the way you have been wonderful to me and *you will always be very special to me. I hope the girls are doing ok. Let them know I hate it that I won't be out soon enough to get to do all the things we wanted to do. But also let them know nothing has changed about how I feel about them. Well, Babe! LOL! I know this may not be the best letter in the world but it's real! Now we can move on! I will be calling you tomorrow and I'm sure we will talk about this some more. Just know that I do love you and need you in my life. I'm not doing this to push us away from each other but only to draw us closer. Tons of hugs and kisses to you. Please bear with me for a little bit and give me some time to adjust. I've got to get my mind back on doing this time and out of the world. You will never ever know how bad this got me! But just know I will be alright no matter what! Baby, you have a great week and good luck on your 2nd test. There's no doubt you won't make it. You're in my prayers always!*

Sincerely,

Bonnie ♥

My child,

Wait with me for a while. I have much to tell you. You are walking along the path I have chosen for you. It is both a privileged and a perilous way: experiencing my glorious presence and heralding that reality to others. Sometimes you feel presumptuous to be carrying out such an assignment.

Do not worry about what other people think of you. The work I am doing in you is hidden at first. But eventually blossoms will burst forth, and abundant fruit will be borne. Stay on the path of Life with Me. Trust Me whole-heartedly, letting My Spirit fill you with Joy and Peace.

Love, Jesus

1 Kings 8:23

Galatians 5:22-23

Just a little letter from Jesus to you. Hope it helps you as much as it did me! You know I can't ever do this without the help of the Lord. So, no matter how mad I get about how things turn out I have to stay in the will of the Lord! May God Bless You Dearly!

Sorry I'm such a mess right now but I guess it's good that you know the good + bad side of me! Love you! :-)

Bonnie sent me a cool picturesque card with mountains, desert plains and a great sky. To me, it was an image of freedom and space, and something she has not experienced in at least three years, yet I was grateful she sent me a card and shared this idea with me.

My Coronado,   *8-26-15*

I wanted to write and let you know that I think you are the best. I have been going thru a real rough time and I haven't always had the best attitude but you have taken it like a champ. You are my other half! I believe that! I have never seen anyone who has put up with me! I really want you to know that I love you dearly! I don't ever want to lose you! You know I really thought you would walk away when I didn't get to come home but you're still here! That has shown me so much about you. I don't love you for what you do. I love you for who you are and how you make me feel. I love the way I feel when I am in your arms. I feel safe and at peace. I don't always know what to say but never think it's because I don't love you. I want this to work more than you. Please have a great day, my Love. Sending Tons of Kisses your way! I love you with all my Heart! Please let the girls know I said Hi, love them and miss them so so much!

Your true Love,

Bonnie

I'm going to be ok. Just give me some time! Love you very, very much!

Postmarked on 10 SEP 2015

My Coronado,

How has your day been? I pray it's been amazing. I was just sitting here thinking about you and wanted to write you a few lines to let you know what's been going thru my mind. You know sometimes I sit here and think about if I will lose you before I get out of here. Sometimes it seems you get tired of the fight and all the times you have to be alone. And I understand that! I'm not saying it's wrong or you shouldn't feel that way. I'm saying it breaks my heart that I can't be there for you in those times. I wonder will you finally give up and move on. I know that I would hate that but I would have to understand. I put myself here and I can't expect you to wait. But then I think about all you are to me and all you have done. You say things that make me believe that you are completely in love with me and nothing would ever change that. You have been more than I could have ever asked for in so many different ways. You have loved me even when I was so unlovable. You have stayed by my side even when I tried to push you away. You have helped me pick up the pieces of my shattered life and began to put it back together again. You have shown me that there are people out there that care, even those that you have never met before. You're an amazing person and I'm not sure how I have ever made it thru all this without you. Just to think you would be willing to put your life on hold to wait blows my mind! I know you could have any other woman in the world and chose me and under the circumstances that I'm in. I also love when I call and you're having a rough day and you yell at me! Not really but it's really cool to know that we can have bad days and know everything's going to be o.k. It's just real life even from in here. You make my life real again! I do love you so much!

Now, I would like to know some of the reasons why you love me so much. What made you know that you truly loved me? I love you on the inside and out. I think you are very sexy and carry yourself very well. Sometimes I think you are too sexy for your own good. I wonder how many looks you get from women as you're walking by. I also wonder how I would take it if I were out there to see it. Thank God I'm not. I'm sure I would make a point to let them know who's you were! LOL! I really do love you so much! I also need you to know I love your girls to death. They are precious and mean the world to me. Y'all are like this perfect little family and it's like y'all have chosen to let me be a part of it and I'm greatly honored!

So, this last month has been a very action-packed month. I am a bit worn out because of it. I feel like I have been at an amusement park and rode every ride a

56

hundred times. My head is spinning, my body is tired and I have to get up and go to work tomorrow. I just want a little rest. A little down time to get myself together. What I really need is you! I'm really going to miss you this week but sometimes we have to compromise. Plus, absence makes the heart grow fonder! I really believe with all my heart that we are going to make it thru this. I'm really super excited about your test on the 15th. I want to be there to share that with you more than you could ever know. You know I've never been around someone who has accomplished so much in such a short amount of time as you. I am in awe of you, Babe! Sometimes I wonder will I be able to keep up with you. Oh no, I will tame you! Just watch and see! I'm pretty sure I will know how to get your attention! I know the attraction between us is so strong that one touch from the other and our focus will be on the other. I can't wait! It's already hard enough to sit across the table from you and not be able to crawl up in your arms. I want to touch you how I want to touch you, when I want to. Maybe that's the spoiled brat in me that's what I want and it makes me mad because I can't have it! :-(Yeah, this is me throwing a fit over you! LOL! Well, Baby, I'm going to get this in the mail! I just wanted you to know how I really feel about you just in case you were wondering! You are on my mind more than you think. Please let the girls know I said Hi. Tell them I want a report on you soon. Babe, do what you're supposed to do. Like eat right and sleep with your machine. That's why you're tired because you are fighting to breathe at night so you're not getting any rest. Do what you go to do. I need you! I love you so much and miss you even more than ever!

With all my heart,

Bonnie

My child,

I am always available to you. Once you have trusted me as your Savior, I never distance Myself from you. Sometimes you may feel distant from Me. Recognize that as feeling; do not confuse it with reality. The Bible is full of my promises to be with you always. As I assured Jacob, when he was journeying away from home unto unknown places, I am with you and will watch over you wherever you go. My last recorded promise to My Followers was: Surely, I am with you always, to the very end of the age. Let these assurances of My continual Presence fill you with Joy and Peace. No matter what you may lose in this life, you can never lose your relationship with me.

Love,
Jesus

Isiah 54:10, Genesis 28:15, Matthew 28:20

Hugs + Kisses your way!

CHAPTER 4:

Necessary Precautions

Postmarked on 11 SEP 2015   Jacksboro, TX

Coronado,   *9-10-15*

    What's up? How's everything going for you? I hope all is well. Well you probably already know about me. By now I'm sure my mom has told you about me. If there is anything that you don't know that you would like to know about me, just ask. All right now, about my mom, I am very protective over her so respect her as a woman and don't let me find out any different. That's the only person that's always been there no matter what for me, and I will risk my life to protect her and take care of her, and she lets me know everything so be cool and I'll be cool. So that's that. She's told me that you came and visited a couple of times which is cool because it helps her pass her time. And the extra mail. I'll put you on my visiting list. I'm doing good. It's the same old, same old in here. Not much to do. All I do is hustle up money to eat. I do a lot of drawing and cards and stuff, make a few dollars here and there to get by, and it helps to pass the time. Oh, the captain said that he was going to put me to work on the mowing crew. But that's about it for me. Don't really know what to write about right now. Don't worry about the handwriting, mine's bad too. Well, tell my mom I'm still breathing. Sorry it took so long to write back. Just didn't feel like writing and her letter is on the way. I'm sending hers out along with yours. Well, I'm getting this in the mail. Thanks for writing and for looking after my mom.

    Peace,

    Raul

God Bless you!

Not only was I protecting myself and my daughters from deception and negative relationships, but Raul, Bonnie's son who was also incarcerated, let it be known that he doesn't want his mother getting hurt and would pay the ultimate price to prevent that from happening. Now that we got that understanding out of the way, we could safely and cautiously proceed.

Postmarked on 16 SEP 2015   GIC

The force of the wind bent the little reed,
but when the storm had passed, the reed stood up again.

I love it when she thinks of me and cares enough to send another Card. So thoughtful!

This was hand-written inside:

My Coronado,

I wanted you to know that I am celebrating with you another accomplishment. Once again, I have missed out on another celebration but I want you to know I'm very happy for you. You're an amazing man that knows what he wants out of this life and goes and gets it. That's just another reason I love you so much. You really do amaze me! Have a wonderful day and know I'm celebrating on my end also.

P.S.

Now what's next? :-)

I just wanted you to know that I was thinking about you on your Special Day!

With all my love,

Bonnie

She also included a note:

Sweetheart,

I wanted to write you a fast note to let you know that I have been thinking about you every day and I haven't called because we are on lockdown. They won't allow us to make phone calls right now but as soon as we can you know I will be on it calling you. I can't believe this happened like this because I wanted to call you at lunch again! Just know that I am celebrating with you, Babe! I miss you like crazy! ;-) LOL! It is almost hard to breathe because I haven't heard your voice in so long. I hope I get to talk to you before you get this but if not, I'm going to need to see you this weekend. On the 20th is pictures. Babe, I miss you really, really bad! More than I can find the words to say. I had you a card made but we are on lockdown so I'm sending you this one instead. Hope you have a wonderful day! Have a blast and don't forget to tell me all about it! Just know I want to be there so, so bad! Hey, let my family know that we are on lockdown please! They surprised us this year so we didn't have a chance to let anyone know we were going down. Let them know I will call as soon as I can. Let the girls know I said Hello and hope to see them soon, also.

I need to get this finished so I can get it in the mail. So, know that I love you really, really bad and I need to see you soon. You know my heart could just stop beating. :-) Just know I need you in my life. Have a great day! Please let me hear from you soon. We still get mail on lockdown! Hint, Hint. Love you, Babe! Congratulations!

With all my Love,

Bonnie

P.S.

Lockdown can last up to 2 weeks. We have never been where we couldn't use the phone that long but they are doing a lot of things different this time. Just please know I love you and miss you.

Update: They just said it might be next week before we get to move to the dayroom. That's where the phones are, babe! If that's the case I need you to come see me please, please, please, please, please!

Postmarked on 23 SEP 2015

My Love,

I'm about to go crazy because I haven't heard from you. I sit here wondering if you got my card and letter. If not I'm sure you are wondering what the heck is going on. You know I have been sitting here all day wondering if you will be here tomorrow for a visit. Can't you tell I'm about to lose it. I can tell you right now that I don't know if I could ever be away from you very long. This is about to kill me, my love. All I can do is sit here and wonder what all the new and amazing things you are doing. You don't have to worry about me tho. I've been right here in this same little space trying to find things to keep me from losing it. You know you can only sleep, read and write so much until you can't do it anymore. I have cleaned every inch of everything I own. My box is about empty because we haven't been able to go to the store and get anything. I'm real hungry, babe. LOL! Can't you tell this little princess is under some stress? It's real real bad, babe! I need you so much right now!

O.K. Now that I have gotten all that out, I need to know what you have been up to. Where have you been and what's been going thru your mind? Please just know I love you! I hate that this has happened like this but we usually have a couple of days' notice to let everyone know. We didn't get any warning this time. And with every other lockdown we have been thru we get to move around the next day or two. Not this time. I'm not sure if you will come tomorrow because you don't know what's up. But I want you to so bad. I'm really about to trip over not hearing from you. I did hear from Raul and he should be writing you soon. He said he's not sure what to say but he's sure he can find something. So, you should be getting something soon. I haven't heard from anyone else. My granddaughter's birthday is on the 24th (that's Raul's little girl) and my middle son's birthday is on the 25th. I just wrote them some letters and sent them a card. I wish I could call home by then to get my family to do something for them. They could go get my son and let me call him this year on his birthday! I don't know! You see all this thinking I've been doing? Baby, I love you and I need to hear your voice. What I really need is to touch you but anything would be better than nothing. Well, I'm going to go for a little bit but I'll write more later. They are talking about keeping us on lockdown until Thursday. HELP!

9-20-15 Well, no you today! I'm just going to say you haven't gotten my letter and card. I hope it's that and not that you're upset with me. Because I have no control over this at all. I can't believe you haven't sent me any mail or come to find out if I'm ok or what! What's going on? Where are you? I'm about to freak out here. I have done nothing but think of you for days now. I've even had to rub a couple out! LOL! But this is the truth. I was looking so good today I was getting tons of comments. Sure wish my baby could have seen me! ▢ Well, Babe, not sure what else to talk about. The air is very tense around here. Everyone is tired of looking at each other. I've had to hold my tongue a couple of times and come sit down. This has got to be a test. I don't know what the test is but I pray I pass! LOL! I know I have done nothing but ramble but this is the only thing that keeps me sane right now. Plus, I miss you so bad I can't hardly breathe. I miss you so much I'm pretty sure I will cry myself to sleep tonight. ☺ This is the hardest thing I think I have ever done. Well, I'm going to go. Write more then! Love you bunches!

9-22-15 O.K. I got your mail you sent on the 14th. The photos of my family and the other goodies. I feel a little better but you sent this before we went on lockdown. I'm still wondering why I haven't heard from you since then. Maybe it's the mail room. Well, Babe, it looks like we are going to be locked down until Monday of next week. I have no food in my box and no money on my books so if you could help me out somehow, I would ever be in debt to you. We go to the store this Friday and then one day next week. Anything would help. I'm going to try and get my family to help out. Thank you for sending me those copies of the photos and my mom flowers if you didn't change your mind. You're an amazing guy. I do love you very much. I'm about to go out of my mind not hearing from you. Please write me or come see me. We are on this strict lockdown because they found a weapon at one of the other units. One person messes up and we all have to pay. I'm a little upset about all of this. Never in my three years have I ever been thru a lockdown like this. I really have to self-talk my way thru every day because after a while you just want to freak out. Hey, also Babe, Tina hasn't gotten her photos back and she was wondering if you sent them back to her. Did you give Pedro her short note? She just keeps asking. I really don't care but please send her photos back to her! I know I'm a pain but that's what makes you love me. I keep you going, right? I miss you really, really bad! I just sent my kids the photos of me. Did you send Raul some for me? I hope so because I told him you would! Thank you with all of my heart if you did. Please let the girls know that I <u>loved</u> the picture they drew of my name. I miss those girls so much too. Let them know I think about them a lot. I hope to see all of y'all soon!

So, what's going on out there in the world? We haven't gotten to hear anything but the radio and they don't say anything. Oh, also one of my bunkies wants to know how you know what you are with the cards. Like how do you figure out that I'm an 8 of Hearts? Can you send us the instruction on it and what they mean? A few of the girls are just curious about it. So, are you going to put the ranch up as a hunting lease? That would be good. You can make some cash off of it. Have you gone to New Mexico to see the other place yet? How's everything going at the lodge? How's work? Tell me what's been going on. You know what I've been up to? Nothing! Just missing you! I hope you got a hold of my family for me so they know what's going on. If not, I'm sure they have called to check on me. I'm sending out letters to everyone because I'm needing some love in here. It's pretty lonely. And you know how busy I keep myself and then they shut me down. Man, it's hard time. Find me something to do, Babe! Please, Please, Please!

Well, I'm going to end this letter and get it in the mail because God knows how long it will take to get to you. You know I love you with all of heart. It's hard to breathe without you! Write me! Oh, and if you would sleep with your machine on, you wouldn't be so tired all the time. I promise you that you would feel much better. If the mask is not that very comfortable get a different one. Just please take care of my baby! You know that I love you real Big! I really want to see you and touch you. You are in my prayers and I pray God guides you and protects you each and every day. I ask that he will bless you so greatly that you cannot understand. Tons of Hugs + Kisses to you!

Yours Truly,

Bonnie

P.S.

I feel like Cinderella and they won't let me out of this evil place! LOL! I will call you just as soon as we come up off of lockdown. Any time of the day just so you will know I will be calling you later on that day. O.K.? Answer me before I think I've lost you!

Dear Child,

I am with you and all around you, encircling you in golden rays of light. I always behold you Face to face. Not one of your thoughts escapes My notice. Because I am infinite, I am able to love you as if you and I were the only ones in the universe

Walk with Me in intimate Love-Steps, but do not lose sight of My Majesty. I desire you to be My closest Friend, yet I am your Sovereign Lord. I created your brain with capacity to know Me as Friend and Lord simultaneously. The human mind is the pinnacle of My creation, but so few use it for its primary purpose – knowing Me. I communicate continually through My Spirit, My Word, and My Creation. Only humans are capable of receiving Me and responding to My Presence. You are indeed fearfully and wonderfully made!

Love,

Jesus

Psalm 34:4-7

2Peter 1:16-17

John 17:3

Psalm 139:14

Postmarked on 25 SEP 2015   GIC

My Coronado,

I know now you have been very worried about me. I got the JPAY you wrote the prison staff. That's my baby. You tell them about themselves! You know I have let them know y'all are all worried about me but they don't care. We are still on lockdown but should be up by this weekend. I hope I get to talk to you in the next couple of days or I'm going to just cry! :-(I miss you really, really bad. I got a letter from my mom yesterday and she was so happy about the flowers I sent her! You are one of the most amazing men in the world! She said they were so beautiful that she couldn't stop looking at them. :-) That really made her day she said. She also said to tell you thank you because she knows you had a hand in it. Babe, you sent them to her like you said you would even after you hadn't heard from me. You just don't know what that shows me about you. I love you so much! Thank you from the bottom of my heart. You are just so great to me! Man, I just can't wait to see you again. I miss you really, really bad.

Today has been a very good day! Today is my granddaughter's 1st Birthday! I haven't gotten to meet her yet. I sent her a card and a letter. I hope she gets them. Raul is very upset about it all. He hasn't gotten to meet her either and now he is missing her 1st Birthday. He will be alright I pray! He's about to be out anyways. He hasn't seen parole yet but I'm sure he will soon. You should have a letter from him by now and he said the phone is not set up. And that's o.k. I also got a letter from my youngest two. Of course, they love me and miss me! They drew me their hands! I miss them so very, very much. They're all going to be grown by the time I get home, Babe! :-(

Well, I was in the Echo (the prison newspaper) and thought I would send it to you! I figured this would be one of those photos you wouldn't ever be able to get your hands on unless I sent it to you! Everyone says that I look so beautiful! I was sitting up all straight and proper! LOL! They were making fun of me for trying to look so cute in a prison photo! I told them I got to look good all the time! LOL! You will never know who might see it. Raul should get this photo of me so you don't have to worry about sending him this one.

Well, I'm going to get this in the mail. I hope you have gotten my other mail by now. Just know that no matter what goes on, I do love you. It may take a minute but I will get in contact with you! Tons of Hugs + Kisses!

Love you deeply,

Bonnie

P.S.

My son's birthday is tomorrow! He will be 16 yrs. old!

I'm about out of stamps and stuff till I get money and we don't go again till next week to the store. So, I'm giving you a heads up if you don't hear from me. I love you lots!

Postmarked on 30 SEP 2015

Tina

I received a letter from her friend, a fellow inmate, to give to my friend Pedro. I didn't read it but it was most likely a request to return photos she had given him. When I asked him about it, he said that he hadn't gotten around to sending back her photos, and I left it at that.

CHAPTER 5:

Firm Beliefs

Postmarked on 08 OCT 2015

Dear Coronado,   *10-7-15*

I am writing you to share with you some of my thoughts that have really been going thru my mind. First of all, it seems the only way I can get you to hear what I have to say is to write you. On the phone you never seem to let me say much and when I do say something you either blow it off or completely avoid it and change the subject back to yourself. I have been going thru hell for a while now. In fact, I have been under so much stress I'm not even myself. But you don't even seem to notice that change in me because of your lack of interest, maybe? I have been acting like a complete fool.

I have become everything I have worked so hard not to be. I have been cussing like whoever and I haven't done that in years. Talking about having sex with other people while in a relationship has been out of the question for years. Now I'm talking about having a girlfriend? I have never in my life done that or wanted to do that. So just know this could never be an option. This is me not being me. I was also thrown off by you sending me $13.00 and telling me to use it wisely. You know, for one, I have never asked you for a thing and when I do this is what I get. First off, things in here cost more than things in the world. So, I'm not sure what all you think I can do with $13.00. I'm thankful but if it was that serious for you when I could have done without. You made it out to be like a burden for you. So, I will not ever go there again. Then the whole thing about the card reading! You acted so messed up over all that and I was only trying to be interested in something you felt was important when in all reality I don't agree with it and don't believe anyone can know my future but God. We have some very different beliefs and I feel this is going to be a major problem in our relationship. I can't say what you have spent 20 years studying is wrong but you can't tell me that what I've spent 38 yrs. knowing is wrong. So, tell me how is this going to work? I know that the Bible is our instruction guide to how we are to live our lives. And that is how I intend to live my life by what the Word of God says. You act like it bothers you that I want to put God first in my life and if that's so, we have another problem. I don't understand why you feel you have to be a part of all these secret societies? You never want to let me in on a lot of things I ask about. I just really feel that I have been 100% with you about me and after the research you have done you *have never found me lying. I know absolutely little about you. You have photos of my family and even had contact with them and I have nothing from you. You want to talk about sex and yes that's all great but check this out, we can't do one thing for each other in the situation we are in. I don't feel right talking like that in a room full of people and when you talk to me like that, there's not much I can do with a room full of people! You don't know my schedule because you don't really care to know my schedule. Remember, I live here doing the same things every day for the last 2 ½ years. I know you have a life out there and I am really glad your life is full of adventures! Really, I am! But this is my life right now! And when I try to share you the things that are important to me, you brush them off. I need someone here to listen to me sometimes, too. You know it has gotten to the point I just don't say anything because it seems to be unimportant to you. So, I just let you say what you feel like you have to say. You know I feel the honeymoon is over for you or have become so busy in your life that you don't have time for this anymore. And that's o.k. I understand! I really do! You know I have really lost track of myself and what I want to stand for. I have become conformed to pleasing this world and not God. So, I will hope you can understand that I'm taking a few days to find myself again. You know in the bible it says if we are not gathering his sheep, we are scattering them. Here lately I have been scattering them and that's not who I am going to be. I have turned my back on everything good and what I stand for and I am not happy with it. I'm a very outspoken person and I have shut my mouth and let things go unsaid. This has only hurt me and allowed me to somehow become bitter and angry. I'm not that person. So, this letter is just to let you know where I stand and what I'm going thru. I'm not sure you care or will ever read this but I have done my part. I'm not, not calling to punish you or to get back at you so please don't personalize this. It's not about you! It's really about me! I'm checking myself and trying to figure out where I went wrong. Because in reality you can only go as far as I will let you go. So, what goes on with me I is what I allow to go on. Look nothing has changed in my plans for when I get out. I'm still going home to see my mom and kids. I want to get my life together. God will and has always got to be #1 and when He's not, I have to check myself. I have to be selfish at first because I have to do what is best for me. I can't continue to just allow things to stay the way they are if they are causing me not to be happy. Now I love you and you are a great person! I'm not trippin' this time. I'm just finding myself and my boundaries again. Let the girls know I said Hi and I'm thinking about them! Maybe you will have time to sit down and think about this and reply. No matter what happens I will be right here doing what I have been doing for years.*

Sincerely,

Bonnie

My Coronado,

Well let me give this a try! You know the last couple of times I have wrote have not been so great! I do want you to know that I do love you and miss you like crazy. But?! No, I'm just playing! I know I haven't written in a while but I just feel like I have written in the world and nothing in return so I'm just a little burnt out. I'm really burnt out on everything. I may be getting a little depressed but I will get thru it soon! I think it's the change in weather. All I want to do is sleep. I also know it's getting close to the holidays and that's a down time around here. Plus, there are a lot more things that go around here than what you know. But I've made it this far and I won't give up now. I wanted to write the girls because I missed them and also because I want them to know even though I'm not there I'm still concerned with what goes on in their lives. They are a couple of very important and special little girls in my life! It puts a smile on my face to just think about them. Yes, Babe, it puts a smile on my face to think about you, too! LOL! They are just a little tiny bit Sweeter than you! You get mad at me, and they don't! :-) I'm very excited to know that you might come see me this weekend. I'm not sure I will know how to act it has been so long! It might be like the first time again. Who knows? Well, my bunkies is all doing o.k. I haven't heard anything from my dad, so that has to be good. My kids haven't written back but I'm sure they are good. My pen went out! Oh, good news everyone is seeing parole 3 ½ months early! So, I'm looking at seeing then again in May. Maybe! That would be great to get out in the Summer. My kids would be out of school and I could spend some much-needed time with them. I will be getting my Associates degree in Bible College by Jan. So those are a few things I have found to get excited about again. Beth should be leaving any day and Linda will leave about Feb so both of my bunkies should be gone soon. So, I will have to meet new friends around here! I'm not real sure I want to do that though. Only time will tell! Well, at least I still have you, Babe. Well, I'm going to get this in the mail so the girls can get their letters. I need you to know that I'm very thankful for all you do. You are an amazing man and sometimes I get caught up in myself and I forget to tell you that. Sometimes I get caught up on "poor me I didn't get no mail, or I don't have money to go to the store" and I forget y'all have a whole life out there too, and y'all struggle, also. I'm very sorry if I have been ungrateful or self-centered. I just sometimes get caught up in the things inside this place and can't seem to see past the walls and this crazy thing they call life behind bars. I'm sure you can tell by my handwriting that I'm not really feeling the whole writing thing right now. But I want you to know that I think you're important enough to write even when I don't feel like it. You are very special to me so no matter what we go thru, just always remember that. I really need you in my life right now. I love you to the moon & back. O.K. so I know you have lots to do with the girls and I know you have lots of pictures to send me. So, I will be waiting on them. Smile! I know I'm a pain in your butt but if I wasn't you wouldn't want me as bad as you do. You know I keep you on your toes and keep you busy! You need that so you don't get old. If we don't stay young at heart than we will give up on life at a young age. I know you're a very busy man but when you think about me just print out a couple of photos and mail them to me! :-) I really miss your face! You know I miss your soft hands and how warm they make my heart feel when I touch them. I miss the way your lips feel when they press into mine! Well, I will stop here because I'm sure you are reading this to the little angels sitting next to you. I sent you a funny (HAHA) out of the newspaper. I thought it would fit us pretty well! I hope you like it. It made me laugh like crazy!

Well, this letter has gone on longer than I thought and it's crazy I feel better than I started. Write me every once in a while, babe! It sucks to never get no mail. Go to the doctor for your hand so you will have no more excuses! LOL! Fix it Babe! You're going to need it! I love you so so so so much! I miss you more than I will ever let you know! Alright, Babe, take care. Sleep with the machine till you can sleep with me! LOL! You're always in my thoughts and prayers! Tons of Hugs + Kisses your way! Catch them and don't let any of them pass you. I don't want them landing on some old lady's backside! LOL! Now that made you smile! Love you bunches!

Always yours,

Bonnie

P.S.

It's one of those cloudy cool days you just want to lay in bed next to someone special and watch movies all day. I know you thought I was going to say something else and I was but I was going to save it for last. But since I already blew it, I guess I will just have to end this. You are that someone I have been thinking about lay next to me all day! Oh, and haven't been watching a movie so I will leave the rest up to your imagination. I love you, Coronado!

Jacksboro, TX

Coronado,   *11-15-15*

     *How are you doing? How are the kids? I hope and pray
that y'all are doing good. I'm sorry I haven't written
back in a while. I got a new job and I got to go to work
at 7:30 in the morning and I don't get back until 6:30 in
the afternoon. I wash all the trash cans in the Unit and
help push the trash to the dorms so they can eat and
whatever else they want me to do. I saw parole and I
should be getting an answer any day now. It's been like 6
weeks since I've seen them. I hope that they will let me
out of here this time. The food here...it sucks really
bad. Everything is turkey based and it all tastes like
shit. But I do a lot of drawing to get some food to eat,
but it's been a little hard because I've got to work all
day and don't have time to draw that much. But it will
all work out. Yay! My mom said something about being the
director of the choir. We don't have things like that. We
barely get to even get out of the dorm just for rec. If
you work the food is brought to the dorms and your
clothes. Everything is brought to you so it's long and
boring around here. They do have a praise on site and
they setup for church and sing a little but I don't like
to be in front of a bunch of people. Well, just dropping
a couple of lines so you can get some mail. I got to go
to bed. It's late and I'm tired and got to get up
tomorrow. Thanks for checking my parole answer and
writing. Take care and God Bless you.*

        Raul

My Baby,   *11-14-15*

   *We just had one of the best visits ever! :-) It was so great that you will have me
praying for another very soon. Mostly so that I will see your sexy self again. Babe,
you're amazing! I really mean that. You make it hard on me because I want to touch
you how I want to touch when I want to. Also, I felt a connection with you that I've*

never had before. I really do love you! With every visit or even phone call it all seems to become more real that you are going to be here with me and do love me. You know I guess I'm so used to having people in and out of my life so much it's just hard to believe there is really someone that wants to be there for me. It's like you're too good to be real. Because I think things don't happen to me like this! But you're still here. This is all really new to me because I get the opportunity to get to know you, (really know you) before I have the chance to get my hands on you. So, this shows me that this just might last for, forever! :-) I hope and pray! I just want you to know that my feelings for you have just went to another level! I really, really love you, Babe. I'm going to go to bed and have wonderful wet dreams about you! Matter of fact, I was just sitting here thinking about when you said you would hold me by my thighs and play with my clit. Well, here's some thoughts I had and I'm about to show you a part of me you haven't seen. My thoughts were of you and me together just lying there holding each other. I would start by kissing you all over. Then I would work my way to your chest. By the way I love a man's chest! :-) I would trace circles around your nipples and gently run my fingers down to your belly button and begin to explore your waistline! I do it with such gentleness that I feel you shiver with each touch. My mouth then begins to place gentle kisses down the same path now sending your body into full motion with each touch of my lips. My hand gets very curious and makes its way down to your hardness! My mind explodes with excitement because I know this is the very thing that I have needed for so long. My mouth finds its way to the tip as I trace my tongue around and around. You now feel my warm breath as I place it in and out. Slow at first which leaves you craving more. Then out of nowhere I take every inch of you into my mouth. I hear a soft moan escape your lips. I feel your hand grab my hair letting me know you want control. So, I raise up as you turn me over and lay me on the bed. From here on out you are in complete control. You start by gently kissing my inner thighs that send chills up and down my body. I then feel your fingers taking their place rubbing my clit. Then your mouth finds it ways to take the place of your finger which sends me over the edge. I'm completely caught up in the pleasure of the moment that I don't feel you change position and begin to stick your hardness inside me. We both are overcome by the moment we have waited for so long before we know it, we explode with a pleasure we have never had before. We then lay in each other's arms!

Alright, Babe, well I guess I will go get in the shower and rub one out! That got pretty intense there! LOL! But now you know what I think about when I think about you. You have always asked now there you have it. And just so you know, it's so much easier for me to write it out then talk about it in a room full of people on the phone! Today I really wanted to eat you up, even more than that cupcake. Now you know that was a lot because I almost got off on that cupcake! LOL! Alright already! I'm going to stop! Sometimes when you get me on a roll I don't know when to shut up. I just want you to know how I really feel about you and when I say I think about you that I do think about you. We are not just friends in my book and I think you have been needing to hear that from me. I love you bunches, Babe. Now don't expect letters like this always.

I loved spending time with you today. You never know how much of a better week I will have because of it. I really believe you love me a lot. I already miss you like crazy. Well, Baby, I hope this next week is a million times better than the last couple. Let the girls know that I'm thinking about them and can't wait to get their letters. I have 10 more days until my 36th Birthday! I keep getting younger and younger every year! :-) Then turkey day and then a month and we will be done with Christmas! Jan. is my month to get the Associate's degree and then I'm out the door! Yeah! Then your Birthday! I hope I can be your B-day present! Just got to keep me in your prayers. Well, Babe, it's been a long time since I wrote you but I believe this will make up for all the lost time. But most of all know that I love you more today than ever and I will love you even more tomorrow. I couldn't ask for a better man. Sleep good tonight with the mask on! LOL! No for real just imagine that it's me on your face and it will make it a lot easier to do. I love you so so much!

Your always,

Bonnie

P.S.

Hey Babe look I need you to help me out of here. I need to get some things from the store. I have been asking my mom but when I do, they ask me if you're not helping me out and I tell then some so they haven't been sending me much because they are not doing so great right now. I don't want to tell them you're not helping because my mom will just go thru her spiel and I don't want them to say anything negative about it because it would really upset me and it would cause problems. So, anything will help, Babe! We go on the 20th and it's the last time until next month sometime. I wouldn't ask if I didn't need it bad! I'm going to go for real this time. I love you so much and can't wait to be in your arms. Life will be so much simpler! Tons of Hugs + Kisses your way!

Hey you can add this one to your shoebox too + tell me about it later! :-)

You can send Western Union you just need my name + TDC#!

Postmarked on 30 NOV 2015

My Coronado,

Let me start out by saying Thank you for the J-pay and the B-day wishes. I was very happy to hear from you. I do love you so very much and I miss you a lot. Also, thank you for letting me know about getting in contact with my daughter. Please let her know I love her and would love to hear from her. She means the world to me. I had a wonderful B-day on Wednesday and a Great Thanksgiving on Thursday. I really did miss hearing your voice but I completely understand what you are going thru. I am praying for your situation to change and that you will get on your feet again soon! I feel I have been a part of your struggles and for that I'm very sorry! I would like to tell you that I know that we made an agreement for me to call the days we did and I would do that just as much for you as for me. I thought you needed it, so I would call. This is what I need you to know: you should have told me weeks ago that you couldn't afford it then we could have cut back then so we would still be able to talk now. I'm not sure if you truly know this but I'm not after anything you have or what you can give me. So, I need you to feel comfortable enough with me to be able to tell me when things aren't so great and we can figure out a way to fix them. If I don't know what's going on then I don't know to change anything. I know you want to be the man and be the provider and it makes you feel bad when you can't. But I need you to know that we go thru things and it's o.k. You know what, I'm right here and will be until God allows me to leave. You don't worry about me but take some time to get on your feet. I completely understand! You get your bills paid and some money saved up! Just write me a letter every now and then to let me know how you are and love me. If you do get the phone on, I think we should cut down to one or two calls a week. I know you love me and you know I love you so we should be good with a couple of calls. I support you in whatever you want to do with the ranch. You can keep it or not. You know what you need to do. Maybe you should focus on your coffee company a little more also. Stop letting me consume so much of your time. I hope you don't resort to stripping but hey sometimes we have to do what we have to do. I really hate that you're going thru so much. It has really brought my spirits down and you know I don't need any help with that thru the holidays. So please get yourself focused on what you need to do. I promise I will be fine in here. You know when you talk about going hunting and buying scopes for your guns, that leads me to believe you are doing o.k. There's just a lot of things that led me in that direction that you were making it just fine. I don't know! I just wish you would be real with me. I feel you hold a lot back from me and then when you let it out you drop it all at once. I have been with money and been without money, I lived with the richest and the poorest and I can say I was happier living the simple life with little money. It's so not about money! If I can't get any clearer then I don't know what to say. So please don't ever be afraid to let me know when you are in a bind. I had a great B-day! Yes, thanks to Linda! She also brought

73

me the J-pay you sent her! I'm not sure what that was about but anyways! Thanksgiving is today and I have nothing better to do but write the man I love and express how I feel! Please let the girls know I'm thinking about them and I will write them soon! I'm just not in the best Spirits right now but I am thinking about them. Please take care of those babies before you worry about anything to do with me! I love you very much and hope you have the best Thanksgiving ever!

Love always,

Bonnie

P.S.

Don't call me Pookie!

Postmarked on 08 DEC 2015 GIC

My Coronado, *12-5-15*

    I know, I'm very sorry I haven't written you all this week but I have been very busy. I have worked every day this week and have come back so tired all I could do is shower, eat and go to sleep. I have also had to double up on my college so I can get it done. But all these are just excuses and I know I should have sent you something. For that I'm very sorry! You are more important to me than any of these things. I want to thank you for coming to visit me. Every time I see you and spend time with you it seems I love you more and more. I think we had an amazing visit and I just loved the kisses! :-) I have talked to my family a couple of times and they're doing great. Mom had to send me an E-comm the other day because I hadn't gotten to the store and I was out of shampoo and some other stuff. Oh, envelopes! That's why I couldn't write also. So, what has been going on in your life? I have not heard from you all week. You must be a very busy man. I pray all is well. I really need to hear from you. I did hear from Casey! Yeah! She sent me the cutest card ever for my Birthday & another one for Thanksgiving! You know I just cried like a baby. Thank you so much for all you have done to help in restoring our relationship! I think you are awesome! I also got a Big Card from Raul! He made it himself! It was the cutest thing ever! I don't know where he got the money to send it because it cost like $2.00 to send it. I didn't hear anything from the youngest three. You know there are young and forgetful. It's o.k. I know they

74

love me. I haven't heard a word from my dad or any of that side of the family. All I can do is pray. The news update here has been good news but maybe not for me. One of the girls here, her mother is the captain at another Unit and she said that Crain Unit has to release 200 inmates by the end of Dec. to meet their quota for the end. I don't think mine will change that fast. One girl here had the answer changed. She was supposed to leave in Feb. but now she will leave any day. WOW! Oh, and in the City of Marlin, TX, they have 2 prisons: Marlin Unit & Hobby Unit. The City has no water so they are having to move the inmates to other units. We are getting some here. I'm sure this will cause an overcrowding issue. So just maybe they will have to release some more of us. :-) Not a for sure thing but maybe a little hope!

Well, it's Sat. and I don't figure you will be here this weekend because you didn't want to take the place of my family if they decide to come. Well. I know they are not coming! It is way too cold and the weather hasn't been so great. So, I'm going to take this time to write letters and send out some of the Christmas Cards I made. Your Card is not the best but I had to make yours. I hope you enjoy it. Oh, these Cards are pop out cards. So, they are made to stand up and look 3D. I'm sure you will figure it out. Please send my love to the girls and let them know we will have fun dressing up your first deer! Let them also know that I loved the Birthday Card – it was beautiful! It put the Biggest Smile on my face! Thank your girls so, so much! Y'all made my day very special! Babe, your card was perfect! Sometimes I don't know what I'm going to do with you. You are truly so good to me. If I don't hear from you in a couple of days, I'm sending out the search team. I love you and I miss you very much. Please let me hear from you soon. I know we have only been doing this for 6 months but you are very much a part of my life and sometimes I feel like I can't breathe without you! I don't like this phone issue but it helps to make every moment count when we have them. You are very special to me. I often think about life after here and wonder how hard it will be to be free and still be so far from you. Will I be able to do it?!?! I really love being with you but I guess we will see how it goes. By then you could have had enough of me and be happy to not have to deal with me anymore! :-(I hope it don't come to that.

So, how's working going? What did you decide to do with the Ranch? Do you miss me? Did you send Raul pictures of us? Have you heard from Casey? What are your plans for Christmas? You know you can't use your hand as an excuse not to reply to my letter because you can go J-pay! :-) Oh yeah! Don't use J-pay to send me money! It is like $9.00 to send it. You can go to Walmart and send it Money Gram for like $3.00. They are trying to rob y'all. My Bunkie told me about it the other day so I wanted to let you know. Hey also when you buy the girls hair stuff, make sure they are black. ;-) And when you look up Tina's photos, it's under Tina Louise Barkley. Well, when can I see your face again? I love you more than I'm sure you would ever believe! I need you in my life! Please let me know you are alive and well! Sending you tons of Hugs &

Kisses. And millions of angels to watch over you all! Be blessed because you are a blessing to me. I love you with all my heart.

Love always,

Bonnie

Thanks for letting my family know Raul made parole! I love you so much + miss you like crazy!

Christmas is right around the corner!

I hope y'all have the best one ever!

I will be back in review at the end of Feb. and should see them again in May! Time flies when you're having fun and living right.

Have a very Merry Christmas! Hope you enjoy the Card!

I love Adele's new song "Hello". Send me the lyrics! Please. Oh, and Stars go Dim, they sing "You are Loved". And also (LOL) That song "Locked Away" I told you who sang it a while back. It says "if I got locked up today and we lost everything, would you still love me the same?" Please, please with sugar on top. Will you send me these? I ♥ u

Smooches!

Postmarked on 14 DEC 2015 GIC

My Coronado, *12-11-15*

 I miss you BAD! I'm trippin' and you know it! I need you really, really bad! This really sucks not being able to hear your voice! Thank you so much for sending me all the pictures of you and the girls! I loved them very much! They make me miss you like crazy tho. I have been very busy but not so busy I haven't thought of you every day. I told Linda that I really miss you I didn't know how much I love you and care about you until now! I have so many great stories to tell you but with each passing day I forget about what happened yesterday and want to tell you about today. But I can never find the time to sit down and write them all to you. We have been working every day and I'm about done with my college! I have really been going hard trying to get it done.

Lots of great parole answers! Some answers have been changed! :-) So there are lots of people in and out of here. I'm really ready to go, Babe! Things aren't getting any better! ☹ Linda has not gotten her answer yet but I'm real sure she's out of here! There's only a few of us old ones left! Just a few more months and I will be out of here!

Please let the girls know I got their letters. And it made my day. Let them know I love them and miss their little faces! Hope y'all have gotten the Christmas Card by now! I'm sending you something else to add to your collection of junk I send you! I just want you to know I love you so much and miss you! I need to hear from you real, real soon. Like yesterday! You know it's easier to get thru the week when I can hear your voice at least once a week! I'm going to go get this in the mail! I want you to know I need you really bad! I love you with all my heart!

With all my heart!

Bonnie

P.S.

So, let me know how things went Sat. with the coffee sales and did you get the power washer? Don't leave me hanging! I need to know what you got going on out there before I really start trippin'! I'm also sorry you had so much trouble when you came to see me last! See that's the stuff I talk about! Be careful, Babe! I care! Don't worry about me I'm really o.k. I just get needy and you're what I need!

Tons of hugs + kisses!

Love you Bunches!

2016

Postmarked on 06 JAN 2016

Dear Coronado,   *1-4-16*

    I know it has been a while since you have heard from me and I'm sorry. I have not been in a good place and didn't want my negative feelings to rub off on you. I just need you to keep me and my family in your prayers. My Dad has been in and out of the hospital for weeks now. He was there for Christmas and New Year's. They have been trying to get me a phone call to him thru the Chaplain but I haven't heard anything yet. He is going to have valve and bypass surgery on Wednesday the 7th. I believe God is going to take care of him :-) I did have a good Christmas! Gabriel, my middle son was at my mom's for a week and I got to talk to him many times and it was truly amazing. Also, he got in touch with Casey and she talked with all of my family. So, God restored all that! He's really amazing. My sister went to go see her but I haven't gotten word yet on how that went. Gabriel tried to call you for me while he was at my mom's but you didn't answer so that was when my sister-in-law texted you about coming to see me. He said you can add him on Facebook and get some of his pictures for me. He is such an awesome kid. I can't wait to get out and kick it with him. He will most likely come to live with me first. Great kid! He's really cool with getting to know you. Raul pulled chair but I have not heard from him. They looked him up online and let me know he's on the move. I'm glad he's almost out of here. I just called home and Casey is moving back to her grandmas. I guess Travis was being mean to her again. My sister went to go see her and grandma was on her way to get her. I just hope she stays away this time. I just got a Christmas card from Raul from the 23rd of Dec. I hope that's why I haven't heard from you. I did get your letter with the Power Washing card in it. I hope your business is going as your job also. I'm really not sure where we are because I feel so disconnected from you the last couple of months. I know funds have been low and things are not how they used to be. I'm trying to deal with all this change but as you can tell I'm not doing a very good job at it. I'm not freaking out or trippin' or anything. I'm just not at a good place. Trying to fight off depression, maybe! I'm just very unsettled, and discontent. You know that this will pass and I will be normal soon. I just wanted you to know what was going on with me. So, you would be trippin'. I love you very much and really, really miss you! I will graduate in about 2 weeks! Yeah! :-) Then I will have done all I can do here. I'm going to need some Word Find or Fill-In Puzzle to do so I won't get bored. You think you can send me some? Yeah, that would be really great of you! I need some kind of a change! Well, Babe, I'm sorry I didn't have a whole lot to say that was good but I do love you and miss you. Oh, I wanted to tell you that Linda got denied parole also. So, she will be here with me for a while. She's been really down also so I'm sure it's not good on either one of us that the other one's down. You know you need someone around to help pull yourself out of the pit when you get there. This too shall pass! Well, write me and let me know what's going on in your life and if you miss me bunches yet or if you have had it with this spoiled brat! Please send my love to the girls and let them know I haven't forgotten about them. I would like to hear what they all got for Christmas. As for you, I really need to hear from you. Tina said thank you for the photos and would love it if you could get the others from Pedro. I don't really care about all that anymore. I would just love to get photos of Gabriel! :-) I need to know what you got going on out there and where are we at? I'm feeling a lot forgotten! :-(Well, I'm going to get this in the mail. So, you will know you're not forgotten and very loved. Don't worry I will be right here waiting on a reply. I promise I won't go anywhere! LOL! Well, Babe, be good and let me hear from you soon. Sending tons of love your way! I miss you and need you really, really Bad!

Yours truly,

Bonnie

Happy New Years!

This is my year to come home! Watch and see! Hugs + Kisses!

Happy 7 months also!

Is the honeymoon over or just beginning? :-) I do love you and nothing has changed on my end! I just love you more & more every day!

Hey, I need you to get Beth's address where she is. I'm about to write her mom and have her send you her letters because mom can't seem to get them into the mail for me. So, look for her to write! Please! With Sugar on top!

My Coronado,   *1-11-16*

    I just love you so so much! I really mean that. I needed to see you more than I thought I did. Man, I love you! Sometimes I wonder if you are really real and if you are, how did I get so lucky to get you?! :-) You know this is how I know God had a hand in this. Seeing you is what I have needed for a while now. I have just laid around all day today thinking of you and how much I truly adore you. I was also thinking about how it took me coming to prison and going thru one of the hardest times in my life to meet the most amazing man in my life! That goes to show you that God turns <u>all</u> things around for our good!

    Well, I called and sang my mom Happy Birthday! It was really late because she was in Memphis at my house getting my stuff. She said there wasn't a whole lot left she found all the things that really meant anything to me. All my clothes were still there but she told me that my fat butt couldn't fit in them anymore! :-(I told her I won't be this big forever! :-) That was some good news! She told me they had to go back and get another load so I guess there is more left than I thought. Yeah! She said the house was not any good anymore! I don't really care. My Dad is improving so much! They said he is doing amazing! Mom went and saw Casey so that was great! They haven't seen each other in years. She's in Memphis at her grandma's.

    That was my life update for you but I'm sure you'll know some of it before you get this! I just want to thank you for all you have done for me and do for me every day! I know you do it because you want to and I am very grateful for that. There are not good men like you left out. Sometimes I have to remind myself to let go of the past and tell my heart to beat again! When I came to prison it has been like I held my breath and won't let myself breathe again until I go home. And to keep from hurting so much I have just stopped my heart from beating! But when I'm around you it's like I can feel my heart beat again. I hope this all makes sense to you because it is hard to explain myself. I just love you and need you in my life!

    O.K. now that you know how awesome and important you are in my life, I really have to ask you a question. Why in the world is it that every time you come to see me here lately, I get a blister on my lip? I just don't understand it! I still love you a lot! We got new mats to sleep on today and I laid down to take a nap and woke up with this thing on my lip! Then I got to thinking this happened before and you said it was from not wiping the can. I did it this time! :-(It will be o.k.! I got mail from Beth tonight. She's doing really great! But she really has much to say. Maybe she will when she gets our letters. She did ask about you, tho! She knows I love you very much! :-)

Now, I'm working on the family tree for you. This should really mess your mind up! Hee Hee! I will try to keep it simple but you know there is nothing simple about me. Oh, and the website is: tdcj-ecommdirect.portal.texas.gov. I think we have figured out that is the cheapest way to send money and that's also the site where you can order stuff. But there is a limit, it's like $65.00 every 3 months if you order my stuff. Mom uses that up when she can. I think I have covered everything you told me to do. Let me know if I forgot something. I'm going to write the girls a fast note. Also, you make sure they know I think about them all the time. I love those little girls to death and I do miss them very much. When you talk to Casey please tell her I love her and miss her bunches. Tell her I need to hear from her. Gabriel, also! Babe, thank you again for all you do! I have many haters because they can't believe I found someone great like you in here! You are the Bestest! This freakin' Guy. Tons of hugs & kisses coming your way! I love you with all my heart and I hope I get to talk to you in a couple of days! :-) Our visit was amazing. I really needed to touch my Baby. Keep me in your prayers as you are always in mine. Keep praying for my Dad. I hope this puts a smile on your face! :-) Because you always put one on mine! Love you Bunches!

Love you with all my heart,

Bonnie

Postmarked on 22 JAN 2016   San Diego, TX

Coronado,

Hey what's up? How are you doing? Hope you're doing good. How's the kids? Well, thanks for writing, and Happy late New Year to you. Yeah, it is a good way to start off the New Year. Yeah, they had me going everywhere from place to place for 2 weeks. I've been to some nice prisons and then I've been to some really shitty ones too and I ended up staying there for 6 days. It was horrible. Rats and roaches everywhere and they didn't feed worth a shit. But I really made it here. It's really a small unit with 600 men. It's pretty nice though and they feed really good. But the only bad thing is that I'm in here with a bunch of people on probation. They are crying about their time, this little old "6-monther" and then you got the ones that think they're all hard. Because they've never been to prison, they just don't know and they think it's a joke. It just makes me mad they don't have respect for one another, or nothing but I just got to make it thru 5 ½ more months. But any ways the weather is nice right now it's about 70 outside which is crazy and there's palm trees and stuff really nice. Thanks for the congratulations on my Baby Girl's birth. Yeah, I can't wait to get out there. That's the only thing that keeps me going. I just got done writing my mom. I'm glad that my sister gave her the gift. That was pretty cool. There's a dude at my other unit who's a pretty cool friend and I was talking to him about what I should draw for my baby girl for Christmas and he just said give me an address and I will send something for you and he came thru. That's what's up. I bet she loved it! I really don't ask people for anything. It's kind of a pride thing, you know? I don't need no help from no one. I got myself in here and I don't expect no one to help me out. Usually I have a hustle but no one here really has any extra money because everyone just got here and getting what they need so my hustle is drawing and I can't make no money if they don't have none, you know? And I am really, really low on hygiene – deodorant, toothpaste and soap so if you can send me like $20? I understand completely if you can't It would help me out a lot. I probably got enough to last me another week or so. And in return I can draw you some drawing for your kids and you, that way you just ain't throwing away your money. Just tell me their cartoons they like or what you want drawn, if you want. Well, man, thanks for writing. It means a lot. I got to get this in the mil so it will go out. Hope you're doing good and your kids.

Raul

Postmarked on 01 FEB 2016   GIC

My Coronado,   1-30-16

I know you have been waiting on this letter for a little bit. I'm very sorry. Just please bear with me and let me get use to my new hours. When we work, we work.

From 7 to 4 we paint the whole time. We stop for maybe 30 mins to eat lunch then it's back to work. Not playing around these days. I went to bed tired and woke up tired. I was so sore I couldn't hardly move. I need a good rub! You think you can help me out? Well, I called you tonight and we had a one-minute talk. It was really great considering the time we had. It was great just to hear your voice. Thank you very much for the money and the e-comm you sent. You will never know how awesome it was to get that. It made me feel really good. I miss you very much. I know it has only been a couple of weeks since I have seen you but it feels like forever. I can't wait to see you next weekend. I have changed a little so don't be surprised. I will go ahead and tell you. I cut my hair! I had to tho because the ends were so dead from all this cheap shampoo and conditioner. To get the food stuff you have to spend $25.00 and I don't get that kind of money. So, I cut the dead ends off about 2 inches. :-) WOW! I know but we will all be strong and it will grow back. I tried to call and talk to you about doing it first but we only had a minute so I made the choice on my own. :-) It's really not that short. Well, I'm not sure what else to say right now so I'll write more later. I love you! Hey there! It has been such a beautiful day! I went out and set in the sun with Linda for a little bit today. Isn't it amazing what a little bit of fresh air and sunshine can do for you? I love it. We even got some exercise! We walked about a mile around the track! You know I haven't really said anything to anyone but I have been very upset because I haven't heard from the 2 babies in almost 4 months. I wrote their grandma a letter and I hope to hear from her soon. I don't know if they got their Christmas cards or gifts from me or anything. It's never been so long since I have heard from them. So, going outside today helped out to get a new focus on some things. I thank God for people like you and Linda in my life. Y'all have been there for me and helped me with some of the hardest times of my life. It makes me see that if you can be here for me thru the hardest time then how amazing will it be in the good times! :-) I really do love you and I'm very grateful to have you in my life. Thank you for all that you do and just for being you. I know I have put you thru the ole Bonnie test and you have come out of it with a shine! You have been very solid thru this whole thing and I love that about you. I don't know what you ever saw in me to be this good to me but I thank God for sending you my way. One day we will have all the time in the world to sit down and talk and you can tell me all about it. :-) We can talk about me, me, me! :-) No just joking. We can talk about us. I hope your weekend with the girls was great! I'm sure I will hear about it in a couple of days. I hope they really know how much they mean to me. I think about them all the time. I wonder how they are doing and what's going on in their lives. Just like I do my own kids! You let them know that. Always let them know that I love and miss them dearly! Let them know that every time I hear from them it makes my week brighter! Tell Veronica I want to hear about her birthday! And Julianna needs to let me know what she has been up to! I think they are some of the most amazing little girls I have ever met. Please give them hugs + kisses for me. If you will ever bring them to see me, I will squeeze them myself! :-) I might even give you a little one, too! I hope that your week was good and the next one is even better! I know mine had gotten to be Last week was pretty rough. I will get in the hang of things again.

I wanted to tell you that I love hearing from you and I would spend all my time with you if I could. Or I would stay on the phone with you all the time if we could afford it but we can't. I promise you that I love being around and getting mail from you more than you could ever know. This is a lot of what keeps me going. You are just so easy to get along with. We just get each other! I love you, Babe Really! A lot! Well, I could sit here and talk about how great you are all night but I'm very tired. So, I'm going to get this in the mail so it can put a smile on your face. I'm sending tons of hugs + kisses your way! So, catch them as they come your way because I would hate for one to slip by and land on a donkey's butt or a toad somewhere! LOL! I love you with all my heart. You are always in my heart and prayers. Have a great week and see you this weekend!

With deepest love,

Your Bonnie

Next time you send an e-comm we will talk about what to send. Some of this was worth the money. So, we will save money if I tell you what I need! I'm not complaining because I'm very thankful. I just think we could get more for the money, that's all. I will let you know. We don't have a lot left on there for a couple of more months. And there are some times we don't get to go to the store for a couple of weeks or more. I might need something then. You are so good to me! Sometimes I don't know how to act. It has taken a lot for me to trust you but you have already proven a lot to me. Love you Bunches!

What do you want for your Birthday, My Love?

Will you get these letters to Beth for us? We sent them to her mom but she sent them back. She's too old to understand. She's like 89 yrs. old. Thank you and I love you so much!

My Coronado,

I hope this will help you feel the love that I have for you. You have totally stolen the keys to my heart. Sometimes I don't know how to react to the feelings I feel but there is no way I can deny them or run from them. You are truly amazing and you complete me in so many ways. I truly believe you are a gift from God. I pray that your feelings and actions will always be real with me. I love you with all my heart! I hope you have the best Valentine's ever! I want you to know you are in my life and that you are my Valentine's! I love you so very, very much and miss you even more! Tons of Hugs and Kisses for you!

Happy Valentine's Day!

Truly Yours,

Bonnie

xoxoxo

Happy Birthday, Coronado!

Hope your Day is the best ever because you deserve it! I'm sending all of my love in this card. It's all I can send for now but just know there is so much more to come!

Happy Birthday, My Love!   *Bonnie*

My Coronado,   *2-21-16*

How are you doing and how are you feeling? I pray all is well. I know our connection has been a little off but I need you to know that it doesn't mean I love you any less. I think about you every day and wish I could somehow hear your voice more. If you want to know the truth, I wish I could see you every weekend and talk to you every day on the phone. I never get tired of you. Sometimes I even get upset because I don't hear from you more or see you when I want to. But I'm trying very hard not to be a selfish brat. I'm trying to put your feelings and needs first. I need you to know that I don't ever tell you not to come because I don't want to see you. It's only because I don't want you to come when you don't feel good or you're not in a position to. I never want to be a burden for you. If it was my way, I would throw a fit and have you come all the time! :-) But you would get tired of me really fast! :-(I love you very much and I know this is hard on you too. If it ever becomes too much let me know! You are already so much a part of my family and life I don't know how I could do this without you. You truly are a large part of what gets me thru each day and sometimes even seconds of the day. I believe you are everything I need and sometimes I think you're more than I need! LOL! You are so loving and caring! I haven't had a lot of that in my life. I don't always understand you or know how to get you to understand me but I would love to spend our lives trying to figure it out. I know you must get very lonely at times but just know that I understand how you feel more than most people. I feel that way most of my days. But please believe me that when I get out you won't have to feel that way. I'll have you so busy you won't have time to be lonely. You will probably get so tired of messing with me you will be praying for some loneliness! :-) I would write you more but I feel like I'm talking to myself. I send out a letter with no reply. I haven't got a piece of mail in 3 weeks! :-(I also don't have much to say other than the same ole things I say in every letter. Even the kids get tired of hearing it. Because they don't write me back either! I even had my feelings hurt when you didn't even send me a card! :-(Sometimes I really wonder if I do love you more! :-) And I have lots of time to sit around and think! One thing I think is that you are truly awesome and I love you lots. You put a smile on my face and make my tummy have butterflies! :-) Yea, you do that! So, you're pretty special to me! With all of this said I want to wish you a Very Happy Birthday! I hope your day is full of blessings! I pray you find so much happiness in this day! You deserve to be happy because you are a wonderful person!

God completely blessed me when He gave you to me. I hope you get all you want for your Birthday! The best I can gave you is this card and me! Hope that's enough! :-) I would love to do more but that will have to wait till I get out of here! If there is something more I can do from here please let me know. I want to know what all you did for your birthday! So that means you will have to write me! Or have the phone working! Baby, I truly love you very much. I could never find the words to say just how much because, trust me, I tried. Love is the most misused word in the English language so it's hard to truly express how you love someone. Just know you are very, very, very, very, very loved! Happy Birthday to you, My Sexy! :-)

O.K. I want you to get a letter that you can read for a few minutes. You said when you read my letters you wished they were longer. So, I'm going to try and do that for you. I owe you a few pages anyways because I haven't been writing as much. Well, first off, I have been going thru HELL! I mean every time I turn around, I feel like I'm running into a brick wall. At work, at the dorm, with Linda, with the officers and my bunkies! WTH! I have had my house trashed more times this week than the whole time I have been here. I have almost lost my job I have had for almost three years. Me and Linda had words that you would not believe. All over some lies our new co-workers said. But thru it all I had God on my side. Every case I was treated with never went thru. My sister (Linda) found out the truth and came and said she was sorry. You know He works all things out for the good for those you love Him who are called according to His purpose. God was there all along all the nights I cried myself to sleep so tired of nothing but hell at every corner. I felt I couldn't get a break nowhere I went. But today things are better! They made me chaplain helper in the middle of all that. I also got my degree. Something I have been trying to do for years. That was a major milestone in my life! I can finally say I accomplished something! Yeah! That was a major deal for me! I have started working out again and feel really good about myself. Last night I called home and talked to my baby brother David for the first time in almost 5 years. It was very emotional but truly amazing. Me and him were very close and this has really messed him up. Me being in here! He said he would come see me soon! I told him I would be home soon so he wouldn't have to worry about it! I also talked to my brother and his wife. It was like our little family reunion! I'm very homesick! I'm so homesick it takes all I have not to cry when I talk about it. I have to take walks or run around the track because I can be alone and cry. I hate being here more now than I ever have. I'm so ready to go home it's about to kill me. I know something good is about to happen because I have been going thru so much. Anyways, Gabriel is supposed to go stay during Spring Break at my mom's house so I will get to talk to him. He's in so much trouble for not writing me! My sister asked about Raul and I told her you sent him some money because he didn't have some things he needed so she's going to try and send him some when her income tax comes in. I haven't heard anything from him. I haven't heard anything from Casey. Mom said she hasn't gotten a hold of them in a while. All I can do is pray for her! You know one day soon I will be home and I won't have to worry about all of this. You will not ever imagine the thoughts that goes thru one's mind that is in here! :-(Well, Babe, I know you don't want to hear this but I'm going to end this to get it in the mail! I want you to get it by your Birthday. And you know how the mail is around here! So, if you get it early just know I know your Birthday is on the 27th. I just wanted to make sure you got it on time! I love you so much! I hope you're not giving up on us! I pray you are just out of sorts because you haven't been feeling well. I do feel something I don't like tho. You don't have to worry about me giving up on you. Babe, have a wonderful Birthday! I would love to be there to make it more special! Maybe you could come see me soon! I would really like that so much! I miss your touch and your smell. I just want to hold your hands and hear your voice. Look in your eyes! I really miss you!

Please send my love to the girls and let them know I am thinking about them, too. I miss them so much, too. You are always in my prayers and thoughts. Tons of Hugs & Kisses headed your way! Have sweet dreams of our life together one day and then write and tell me all about it! I love you bunches!

Love always,

Bonnie

P.S. Smile! You are loved!

Let's not start talking about parole or when I'm coming home. It makes it harder on all of us! Let's just take it one day at a time. And if you can't do this anymore then let me know. I don't want you to do this because you think you have to. I want you to do this because you want to and this is what you want! This is what I want, so don't be trippin'! :-) You are the BEST!

I can't wait to hear back from you! Soon! :-)

1 Corinthians 13 will tell you what real love is! :-) Do you love me like that?

My Coronado,   3-4-16

   I wanted to send you a fast note to let you know I love you and miss you like crazy!
I also want you to know we are on lockdown! I should see you this weekend and I will
tell you all about how much I love you then! But in case you forget, here are a couple
of "Love Is..." to remind you! Please let the girls both know that I'm thinking of them!
Tell Julianna I send all my love in her card and I hope she enjoys it. Let Veronica
know that even tho it's not her birthday, she's still special. Babe, have a wonderful
day! I hope to see you before you get this! I really, really miss you! I love you with all
my heart!

                                                        Love always,

                                                        Bonnie

P.S.

I hope we are only down a couple of days! So, put money on the phone so I can call
you when we come up! Love you!

In her letters, she started to send me comic strips that were created by New Zealand
cartoonist Kim Casali, titled "Love Is...", and it spoke to me more than any *Garfield*
or *Archie* comic did.

Postmarked on 21 MAR 2016

My Coronado, 3-19-16

I think you're one of the most sexy and awesome men I know! I think you're beginning to understand how I feel about you and this is only a small amount compared to how I truly feel! :-) I do love you more than words could ever express.

Here I am writing you a much deserved and needed letter because you have truly been on top of my mail this last week. You would not believe what a difference it makes in my life! :-) Thank you so, so much. You know it's like Christmas when you get mail here. You can't wait to run back to your bed and open it up to see what's on the inside. You could have heard it a million times but each time it means little more. It's like adding fuel to a flame. It makes it bigger and bigger It's also been very nice to hear your voice when I want to. You keeping that phone on has been a gift in itself. I love to hear your voice. It helps to calm me down and it gives me peace on those crazy days. And I just love to hear how your days go. It somehow helps me feel connected in your life more than I am.

Well, I have had the opportunity to talk to Gabriel every day this week. You know that is bitter-sweet. I know he's great and has turned out to be one amazing kid. I just want to be there for him. And only getting to talk to him every 3 or 4 months really sucks. But I thank God I get to talk to him when I can. I need you to get some pictures off his Facebook. If he doesn't have any on there then send him a message and ask him if he has any he wants to send. He will reply to you. He just forgets because he has his head in those video games every spare moment of the day. He is a gamer and always has been. That's what he's going to do in college! :-) I have not heard from any of the others. Casey's grandmother hasn't even written me. That's not normal. So, God only knows! All I can do is pray. Her Birthday is next month along with Raul and Jack's. So, I'm concerned what all she will be up to. She will be 20 yrs. old. Gabriel is 16, Jack will be 13 and John just turned 10. Anyways, the next month will be a little emotional for me with all these birthdays. Just letting you know! Warning!!! LOL! No, it makes me sad that I can't be there with them but I don't want to turn the days of their births into a day of sadness. I'll be strong! So please let the girls know I love them and think about them all the time. They are some precious little angels! I'm going to have a blast with them when I get out of here. A BLAST!

You are supposed to be here tomorrow so I'm sure we will have much to talk about! I love when I get to see you. I can look in your eyes and know what you're saying is true and sincerely from the heart. It changes everything when we are face to face and can touch each other. It makes it real! When we write we can only guess each other's emotion because we can't see the other's expressions or body movements. When we are in person it becomes real! So, I'm going to wait and send this off after our visit. If you don't come, I will write you and let you know how I feel about it! :-) I love you so very much!

Oh, Babe, I just heard our song! I really do miss you a lot! I should be there! I really should be. I often think of how our days will go when we are together. What will we do and how many things will we have in common? How many things will we learn from each other and what things we will learn to like in order to make this work! It's going to be an adventure but a good one. We can say we took our time to get to know each other first! LOL! I love you and I just wanted to let you know I heard our song And I was thinking of you! Tons of hugs and kisses! Xoxoxo

Alright, Babe. You said you weren't coming tomorrow and I'm sad but I can understand. You are the Best anyways. I love it when I get on the phone and you're in a good mood even when you're headed out the door to work. I can't wait for the day when I'm there to kiss you goodbye to head out to work. I would spend the whole time you're gone preparing for your return so that I could rock your world. I can't make it too fun or you might not ever want to go to work. That will have to be your reward for a hard day's work! :-) I love you, babe! I'm going to get this in the mail because you are a letter up on me. How did this happen?!? LOL! I hope y'all have a wonderful Easter! Please tell the girls! I love you to the moon!

Yours truly,

Bonnie

Child,

Rejoice and be thankful! As you work with Me through this day, practice trusting and thanking Me all along the way. Trust is the channel through My Peace flows into you. Thankfulness lifts you up above your circumstances.

I do My greatest works through people with grateful, trusting hearts. Rather than planning and evaluating, practice trusting and thanking Me continually. This is a paradigm shift that will revolutionize your life.

Jesus

Philippians 4:41, Psalm 95 1:2, Psalm 9:10

Just a little food for thought for the day! Hope it helps you in some way! May God bless you day like never before! He takes us from Glory to Glory! Love you!

Babe,

I slept in again this morning. Man, it feels great to get some much-needed rest. I know they have worked us to death here lately. I don't know if I told you that we have a new boss. He will only be working Mon-Fri so we get a 3-day weekend! I'm very excited. More time to get myself ready to come home. Before you know it, I will be out and you won't know what to do with me. Really, I'm not so sure I will know what to do with you! I might even have stage fright! It's hard to sit here and believe I have been locked up for almost 4 yrs. I'm scared I won't know what to do with myself out there. There will be so much that is new it's going to freak me completely out. I will most likely trip out when I go to the store for the first couple of times and have a choice in what I can get. I think about all the struggles I will have to face and if you're going to be able to handle me. It's going to take me some time to adjust to things again. Will we have built a bond strong enough to hold us together thru this challenge we are about to face. I think so, but I often wonder are you going to be as understanding when I'm out there? I hope so because I'm going to need you to be. I'm saying and thinking all this because I know I'm coming home soon. I don't mean to get your hopes up or anything. I just know I am. I've never had a peace about it like I do now. I know I said we were not going to talk about it but I just need you to be prepared. I'm not scared or worried because I know God works <u>all</u> things out for good. So, I know whatever happens it's for my good! :-) Just like you being in my life. God knows what He is doing. Everything's going to be fine. I'm just a thinker and try to prepare to myself. I'm not good with change or surprises!

We are going to have a blast together. You have no idea of how much energy I have and how much fun I can be. I guess you can tell that I love pictures! So, get ready to have your pictures taken at all times. They are memory keepers. You can always look at a picture and go back to that time. I love that.

One thing I really want to do when I get out is to find out how I can come back in but on the other side. I really want to come in and give these ladies hope like so many have done for me! You can come if you want to but you don't have to. I have to do it. It will also be a reminder of why I never want to come back. It only takes one wrong choice that can start the downward fall. I'm coming back! But for the right reason this time. I know my family will support me 100%. I know people that come here from Memphis. They used to be my sister's neighbors. I don't know why I'm telling you all this but I guess it's going to be a part of my life. And if you're going to be in my life the way we both want you to be then I guess you should know. I want you to be by my side because you will be part of my testimony. How we met in here thru it all and we are happily still making it! I know Raul and Casey will be a part of it sooner or later.

Well, Babe, our lives are just about to begin. Are you ready for this? There is so much out there I need to do and want to do that it's kind of overwhelming. I'm ready tho. So, what are your thoughts on all that? I also wonder about how it will feel when you can really wrap your arms around me. Or how it will feel when you can really wrap your arms around me? Or how will it be to kiss you the way I want to kiss you. To feel you touch me in places that haven't been touched by anyone in years! :-) I also wonder what you're going to say when you see me in regular clothes with my hair done and real make-up on. Or when I'm all natural just getting out of bed. You really have never gotten to even know my body movements or really how I walk! Man, you don't know what you have coming to you. I'm a very touchy person. I have to be moving all the time! You will see! Man, this is going to be fun! I can't wait.

So, now can you see what a deep thinker I am? I think about everything all the time. You are a bigg, biggg part of it. I also wonder how you and my kids are going to get along. They will always respect you because of me. But will y'all let your guards down enough to really get some kind of bond? I know the girls and I will have no problem. But my kids have been thru so much more! It's going to take a LOT of work. I'm ready to face it tho. If God is on our side, then we have it made.

I know this letter was on a deeper level than ever before but it's real. These are things we need to prepare for. You will find I'm a problem solver and a peacemaker. I want everything to run smoothly and when it doesn't, I go into and fix it. So, I'm trying to fix everything before it ever starts to happen! LOL! Well, I'm going to get this in the mail so you will have a little piece of me to take with you thru out the next week. I rubbed this letter all over my body so you could have some of me! I'm sending you all my love and bunches of hugs & kisses! Keep me in your thoughts. Love me as much as I love you! Oh, never mind that's impossible for you to do. Keep me in your prayers as you are always in mine. Sleep with the angels and have sweet dreams!

Truly Yours,

Bonnie

You better come next weekend. You're not going to start this mess about telling me you're going to come and not come again. Remember Happy Wife, Happy Life! I promise I will make you the happiest man alive if you will keep me happy. I don't ask for a lot so when I ask for something, I really need it. <u>Remember that!</u> That's an important chunk of information about me! And if I need it, I will find a way to get it. I may be a little spoiled brat but I'm working on that! I'm not perfect, that's Jesus! I'm a work in progress! Keep me happy and don't let me down. I love you even with your farmer's tan. I <u>need</u> my pictures <u>now</u>! LOL.

I hope this put a smile on your face! You put one on mine! Smooches for you!

Postmarked on 29 MAR 2016

My Coronado, 3-27-16

I just wanted to write and let you know that you are on my mind. I love you dearly and miss you more than words could ever say. I know I say this often and over time when things are said often then the impact of what is being said soon fades into something of less importance like Hello, or How are you? I don't want it to ever come to this with you. Every time I say it, I want something inside of you to just explode with joy! :-) Or even something new to happen each time I say it! Let's try it. Babe, I Love You! Did it happen? Well, we will work on it.

Today is Easter Sunday and I have had time to really grab a hold of the true meaning of this holiday. It is a time of new beginnings and new tomorrows. We can step out of who we have been & become this new person God created us to be. I know we have had many talks and we have discussed what a spoiled Brat I am. The reason it seems this way is because I hate change. It used to be my best friend but know I don't like change. Maybe because change in my past has resulted in bad. When things stay the same, I get in my comfort zone and learn to roll with the punches. My life has completely been turned upside down. I'm not saying in a bad way but I'm not sure about all of things at this point. You know my job situation has changed and this could very well be for my good. The Bible College I am in have really been treating me in a negative way. I'm not even sure why. So, I'm sure I will remove myself from there soon. Also, this Chaplain helpers position I'm in has caused some bad waves with me and the officers. I'm not sure if I'm really where God wants me to be. I'm thinking very seriously about getting out of it. So, there I will have all this time on my hands. But maybe that's what God wants for me right now. Maybe I need to sit down without any distractions to think about what my future holds. What I want when I walk out these doors. You know I have a chance at a new beginning. I get to start my new life over and I can do whatever I want or have whatever I want I just have to use my head and make the right choices. So, this Easter has made an amazing impact on my life. I can say I will always remember it.

When I think about our future, I think about the things I feel freely to talk about and then there are those things that just about kill me to talk about or even ask about. But I have often wondered many things that will affect our future. For one: now this is hard for me to talk about because I don't want to offend you or hit a nerve but I have come to a point I have to know. I wonder why you don't help me out more in here. Is it because you don't have the money to take care of me and yourself? Is it because you are afraid to invest anything in me right now because you don't know where our future will go or is it simply because it slips your mind? You have always known that my

95

family does what they can and sometimes I have to do without until the next time. It just has me wondering if you can't help take care of me in here, what's going to happen when I get out? I know I will have a job and will do my part but it's one of those things that just runs over and over in my mind. I don't ever ask you for anything because I never wanted our relationship to be based on what you could give me. I wanted to show you that no matter what we went thru we would be able to work thru it. Now you know I'm a spoiled Brat and I need things! :-) I'm not asking for diamonds and new cars here. I'm just asking for some soap, paper to write on and even some pens. Every once in a while, a Dr. Pepper and some cookies would be amazing. I will save the diamonds and new cars for when I get home. Which will be soon so start saving up! LOL! I say all this to say this, it's hard to ask you for anything. Maybe it's because I don't like to hear no or if it's because you have made it seem to me that you struggle in that area a lot. I just don't want there to be things that you wonder about but feel like you can't talk to me about. Another thing is your family. Why do you not talk about your family much and why don't y'all get together during holidays and special occasions? Is it because y'all have just not ever been a close family or are there issues there that cause y'all to be distant? I wonder these things because I love my family and we have get-togethers just to get together and I don't want that to be a problem. I wouldn't and can't have it any other way. I would want your family to be a big part of your life just like mine is. If it's a hard subject for you then that is o.k. but just let me know that. If we are going to be together these are things we are going to have to work thru. :-) When you were in school were you bullied or the bully? Did you do well in school or struggled a lot? I can say that I was picked on a lot in school. Not until my High School years did I become very popular. I didn't do just amazing in my grades, but even went to Special Education for my reading. But I always did have passing grades. I grew up in a farm that my grandmother owned. My mother farmed it for years. We lived in houses that my mother rebuilt with her hands. My grandmother was a very God-fearing woman and she was disabled most of my life. We spent many days caring for her. She was an amazing woman that taught me so much about God and about life. We were unable to watch TV at her house or play cards because it was a form of gambling and TV taught you things that were not of God. We never had expensive clothes or any of the newest toys. We lived with the things we had to have. It was a simple life but some of the best years of my life. I spent a lot of my childhood life building clubhouses out of scrap wood mom would throw out from building our houses. We would build them in the tree line near our dirt road so we could see everyone coming and going down that road. It was a washboard road that would share every piece of your car when you went up and down it. So, we always knew when someone was coming. The way mom would get us to come in was to holler for us or go out and honk her car horn. We would know it was time to come in and eat or get ready for bed. Good times! So, there's a bit of my life. Some things about me you didn't know. You're always asking! So, I want to know some stuff about you. I'm not as spoiled as you thought! I know how to be content in all things! In here it's a little different. We learn to live with nothing in here. So, the things we are able to get we grab on to because they are very important to us. We are stripped of everything when you walk in here. You don't even feel like a woman anymore. So, anything that you can get to help you get some of that back is a blessing and it hurts to give it up. We don't get good smelling stuff to make us feel like a woman unless we have the money to buy it. So, I'm not being a brat or just want to feel like someone. Green bars of soap don't smell good and they dry your skin out! :-(:-) I love you and need to have you in my life. I also need to know my life will be secure. I need to know where you are at in life and where you plan to go. I think we could do amazing things together but we do have to learn to communicate! You are my future and there are so many things I don't even know about you. I still love you and I'm willing to figure this all out. Can you see what happens when things start getting real? I never shut up! LOL! And you get books to read! There are many other things I wonder about but I will give you small amounts at a time. I just want you to know that I think you are truly awesome! I may have truly met my other half. You are the only man I have ever known that can deal with me and handle me in such a way that just keeps us going. You are just perfect for me! But why me, Babe? There are so many others out there, so what keeps you waiting on me? But send my love to my little angels! Tell them I love the pictures of them in all white washing the car! Very cute! Let them know I miss them very much. Well, I hope y'all had an amazing Easter! I spent it thinking about y'all! :-) Keep me in your prayers as you are always in mine. I hope this letter was received with all the love I put into it with nothing more or less. Please send pictures of Gabriel when you can. Come see me soon! I need to touch you! I love you to Pluto! Tons of Hugs and Kisses!

Love you always and forever,

Bonnie

P.S.

Man, before you could get the first deep letter replied to, I already have you another one on the way! No, I'm just really getting serious about my future and those that are in it. That's you! My Love!

Can't wait to hear from you soon! So, everyone thinks you are very sexy! So, I had to take the photo down! I was getting a little upset with all the attention you were getting. It's for my eyes only! :-) I love you lots!

How's the painting coming along? How about your job? Did you quit? Do you miss me like I miss you?

Dear Coronado,   *4-25-16*

I hope this letter puts a smile on your face. I just wanted to write you a note to let you know how much I love you and miss you. I know a lot of times I get caught up in myself and what's going on to <u>Me</u> in here and I don't get caught up with what's going on to <u>you</u> out there. I'm very sorry. Sometimes I have to slow down and think things thru. I've had a lot on my mind here lately and I've just been a little disconnected to this world. I guess more because of my father's passing. I just wanted to think about other things and keep my mind busy so that I didn't have to deal with it. It's still real hard to imagine I will never see him again while I'm on this earth. But anyways, I've just got a lot to think about. What I'm going to do when I get out. If I'm going to be able to handle everything I need to deal with when I get home. Or even what is it going to feel like to be free again. I'm just trying sort thru some things. I just want you to know that I love you very much. I do care about what's going on with you.

In here we call it "short timin'" when you start doing what I'm doing. We start "short timin'" right before you go home. It's like I'm losing track of time. My days are running together. It's good tho because time is flying. You know I'm not being distant because of any reason that has anything to do with us. I've been very homesick here lately and I'm sure that is why I have been calling more than before. I know it sounds like I'm a mess but really, I'm good. Just feel like I don't have much time to get it together. I'm o.k. and I don't need anything but your love and support. I hope your week has been better than the last. I really feel bad about not understanding the concern you had about the flooding. Please forgive me! :-) You voice puts a smile on my face and it helps me drown out the worries in my mind when I talk to you. Sometimes I don't hear the concern in your voice when we talk. Well, Babe. I know this isn't much but you have been on my mind. I was writing all the kids and the rest of the family and I thought, how could I not write my #1? You are a big part of me and everyone if else can get a letter, you most definitely must get one! :-) Keep me in your prayers and know I love you no matter what. Just know I got a lot of things to work thru in my mind right now! The first I want to do when I get out is go back in school! :-) Just some FYI.

Alright, I'm going to close for now! There is a ton of my love in this letter and I hope you felt it when you opened the envelope! :-) Please hang in there with me! I'm just trying to get it together. Let the girls know I have never forgotten about them and I miss them more than words can say. I would love to hear from them sometimes. I love you to Pluto! Tons of hugs and kisses! May God bless you dearly!

Yours always,

Bonnie

P.S.

Hey, if I sent some pics of my dad to you could you make copies and send them right back? My sister wants them but they are not good at getting nothing to me. I just don't want to be without them very long. They are all I have left of him. Oh, and check Gabriel's page because he is going to try and post some photos. Maybe! Thank you so much for all you do & just for being you! I ♥ u!

Today is Jack's B-DAY!

Postmarked on 12 MAY 2016

GATESVILLE INSTITUTIONAL PAROLE OFFICE

3406 SOUTH STATE HWY 36

GATESVILLE, TEXAS 76528

STATE OF TEXAS

BOARD OF PARDONS AND PAROLES

May 05, 2016

Mr. Coronado Borgia

Re: Wright, Bonnie TDCJ-CID #6497319

Dear Mr. Borgia:

This is to acknowledge receipt of your correspondence dated April 27, 2016.

The information you provided will be placed in the offender's permanent parole file to be available for consideration by the parole panel at the appropriate time.

Respectfully,

L.W. / C.G.

IPO II / Assistant Regional Supervisor

Cc: File

Postmarked on 24 MAY 2016

Dear Coronado,   *5-22-16*

I hope this letter finds you well. I do have to say I am a little concerned. When I talked to you last, I know you said you would have money on the phone by Friday and here it is Sunday. I know you don't lie to me so that is why I am concerned. I can understand unexpected bills or expenses and I'm going the believe that this is the reason. I just wanted to let you that I love you and miss you. I need to hear from you to let me know you're alright. I do have to say when it seems like when I need you the most, something like this happens. I guess this is God's way of letting me know that I need no one but Him. I'm not saying I don't need you, I'm just saying we can't always depend on man but sure can always depend on God. I'm just saying all this to say there are so many things I needed done for my parole interview coming up and you know how my family is. They haven't even have sat down to write support letters. I need pictures of me and my children and family. I'm told I need to make it more personal for them. The only photo they have of me is the one on my I.D. and who would want to parole that?! :-) I did call my sister yesterday and cry to her about it so maybe she will understand how important it is. I just sent off my own support letter and some of my certificates and my degree. It's very close to the time for them to vote. So, so close. I can feel it so I'm very anxious! One of the ladies that saw them with me last year got a parole day-in a couple of days ago. But I need to just give it to God and stop worrying. He's got me! I have been off of work the last 11 days and I'm ready to go back. My time is going so slow. I need something to keep my mind busy. I've read about 4 or 5 books and wrote letters. I had it out with one chick in here that has a crush on me. I had to tell her to stay the hell away from me. Ugh...But I had a good Sunday! I went to Church and it was amazing! :-)

One of the ladies that lived across from me went home a couple of months ago. They told us she passed away a couple of days ago. It's crazy. You just don't know how important every moment is. You never know when you will have your last one. So, we have to find the good out of every moment, even when we might be going thru hell.

I have not heard from anyone in a couple of weeks. As a matter of fact, I haven't gotten mail in 2 weeks! Raul should be getting out any day now and I haven't heard from him since right after my dad passed away. I'm starting to get a little concerned. My mom is still in Odessa. Everyone in Pampa is doing good. So how are you and the kiddos doing? It would be great to hear from you. I pulled out all my pictures earlier and was missing y'all really bad! I would like to have you send me a couple of photos of you and the girls to send to parole if you could. And send some of me and my kiddos off my Facebook. I need them by early next week if you could. I know I ask a lot from you and I'm very thankful for all you do, Babe. I know I can be a brat sometimes and I'm sorry but you will learn to handle me! :-) Well, Babe, I hope when you get this letter it brightens your day to know that I was thinking about you. To tell you the truth I feel really lost without you. I feel really out of place here also. I'm just lost! :-) No really, really, I feel like I don't belong. And that's because I'm about to be out of here! :-) Well, I'm going to go get this in the mail in hopes I will hear from you very soon. Just never forget I love you and I miss you very much! Please let the girls know the same. Y'all are always in my prayers. Babe, I love you to Pluto!

Yours truly,

Bonnie

Hey, do you still have the pics that I sent you of my kiddos when we first start talking? If you do, will you please make copies of them and send them to me for parole?! Please! I'm just trying to get out of here! Smooches!

In 10 days, we will have been together for a whole year! :-)

12 months you have put up with me! I ♥ u Babe!

Chapter 6:

Summer Sizzle

Postmarked on 09 JUN 2016   GIC

Coronado,   *6-9-16*

    Please help me understand something! I don't understand why there are photos of you and some woman on Facebook going to a music concert! That seems very strange that it has been a month since this happened and you have not said a word to me. For one, I told you from the beginning that I know it gets lonely out there and if you ever found someone else just let me know. I could never make you wait for me. That would be so unfair. And for two, if she was just someone that went with you so you wouldn't look alone or maybe she needed a date. Why didn't you say something to me about it? I may be in prison but I'm still alive and breathing. I do have feelings and they do matter. I feel it was important enough to you that you put it on Facebook for all the world to comment on. What a great couple y'all were and how you looked good when you clean up. You were cleaned shaved and all. Well, I wouldn't know because I haven't seen you in months. You would have to know that my family would see it and would be sure to let me know. Even including my children that I don't even get to talk to very often. So, when I do talk to them, they want to know if we are still talking because you are on Facebook with some other lady! I'm very confused and hurt. I have very bad trust issues and you know this. So please help me understand why you waited this long to mess things up or has this been something that has been going on? You have had plenty of chances to say something to me over the last few weeks but you haven't said a word. It just seems strange that you become distant and this happens. It's o.k. Just be honest about things. You don't have your second job so I thought you would have more time to write or even answer the phone when I call but it seems why I'm getting less and less. I'm o.k. tho. I am used to these kinds of things happening to me. I know how to get thru them. I just thought there was more to us than all this. You have to remember I can't see what goes on out there from here so I have to live life thru someone else's eyes. Sometimes that's a scary thing but it's all I got right now. So, all this being said please help me understand what is going on out there. I can't call because I am not in the right state of mind to talk about this in front of tons of other people. You know the fastest way to get a hold of me if you even want to take the time to reply to this. I'm very lost and hurt right now!

Bonnie

This is the kind of things I'm scared of when I get out! Life is too short for all this hurt and pain being in relationships that don't last. I'm tired of the same old patterns. I deserve better than to keep being hurt!

Postmarked on 17 JUN 2016

We hadn't written in three months. I felt we reached that moment where jealousy and misunderstanding commandeered our relationship, and it was a defining precipitous event that may have damaged it, there on out. Where she may have embraced the notion of someone else being in my life, because of her past relationships, I was merely out with friends and it was taken out of context. It was extremely unfortunate but nothing we could not rectify, or work on, together.

One situation that may have helped in rebuilding our friendship is that her son, Raul, was transferred to a halfway house just a fifteen-minute drive from me and I reached out to him to meet for dinner, on September 2, 2016. We met up at the Burger King around the corner from his residence, and he brought along a friend, who I didn't mind, but after hanging out for about an hour or two he turned out to be a real cool young man with lots of ambition and drive, who also recently became a father. I called Bonnie that night and gave him the phone, and it was probably the first time they had spoken in about a year so she was grateful for the connection. She was still his mother and she chastised him for smoking a cigarette while they spoke. *Family.*

My Coronado,   *9-17-16*

How have you been? I hope and pray all is well in faith and health. As for me, I'm at a strange and uncertain place. I'm not saying it is an unhappy or bad place. It's just a place I have never been here before and I'm just trying to work thru it the best I can. My mind is in a million places and life is all about to change for me. I'm just not sure if I'm prepared for everything. You know by now I hate the unknown and change is something I'm not used to anymore. And both of these things are what I'm approaching. I know it's all for the good so I must embrace it! :-) Raul will be home in 7 days and I'm very excited for him. I know he will do great! He's got a good head on his shoulders and he's just like his mom. Very strong-minded! :-) I hear my daughter Casey is doing great. She is staying clean and she even called Raul on the phone the other day! I'm really proud of my kids. They are all doing so well. Plus, they know mom is on her way home and they better get it together because Momma don't play! :-) We have not worked in days, or should I say, in a month or more and I'm about to go out of my mind! You can only sleep, eat, workout, read and listen to the radio so much before you're done with that all. Now all we do is sit on the picnic tables outside and look out into the sky and think. That's not always good. The mind is the devil's playground. I'm just ready to pull chain and get this started so I can get my life back. But we all know that because I've said it in a million times. So that's all I have! :-) What has been going on in your life? You seem to be a whole lot happier. I guess the new job has helped with that a lot. You seem to have more time for yourself and the girls. That's always a plus!!! So here I am writing you and I'm really unsure where we are. You know we're getting along great besides some ups and downs and then you're gone for a couple of months and then here you are. Well, I do have to say I had given up on us and prepared myself to move on. I have to say I was pretty hurt over the whole deal and I put those walls up again because being hurt builds walls. :-(

I'm sorry about this because I know you wanted to keep everything positive but there are just some things you can't just sweep under the rug and like it doesn't matter. I love you and would never hurt you and I feel I deserve the same respect. You just have to know you can't just pop in and out of people's lives when you want to and think it's o.k. I mean would you like that to happen to you? I'm just real guarded right now because I don't know if you're going to do it again. So please understand how I feel. I'm just trying to work thru this. It's been really great to hear your voice again and to know you're doing good. I have also missed seeing you and spending time with you. You have always been able to make me laugh and help me thru some hard times.

You're also a pain in my ass sometimes!! :-) It was wonderful to hear the girls' voice again and to know they are also doing good. Give them hugs + kisses for me! So, April is around the corner! I'm so ready to be home! I can't wait to eat salad and bacon. Take a bath! :-) Sleep with a pillow! Hold my children in my arms for days! :-) Meet my granddaughter for the first time! :-) I'm ready just to live again. To be a human! There will be so much to do and not enough time to do it. I'm just very excited!!!! Well, Babe, I'm going to get this in the mail because you have been expecting one for days now. Please know that I love you and miss you so very much! Thanks for always being there when it mattered the most. And thank you for allowing me to connect with my son again after some years. That meant so, so much! Well, I hope to hear from you soon! Take care & God bless!

Yours truly,

Bonnie

P.S.

I'm sorry if I feel distant. I just have a lot going on in the head of mine. You could begin to understand the depth of things that are going on up here. This is my one and only chance to get it right and there is no room for error. I do love you and miss you lots! Hugs + Kisses!

Linda should be home in less than 30 days! She is so excited! I should leave any day now. You will be able to tell on the computer. It will show my new Unit. And plus, I won't be able to call for a minute. I ♥ u!

Chapter 7:

Burnet, TX

Bonnie transferred from Gatesville, her home for the past four years, and now started to write to me from the half-way house in Burnet, TX. Upon receiving her first letter, I noticed something peculiar about the stamps that I hadn't noticed before. Every one of her stamps that she had sent me were on the right-hand corner of the envelope but were affixed in a diagonal position. I was always used to licking the back and slapping it on right side up, but apparently the way a stamp is positioned holds a different meaning. Interestingly, I sensed something was different.

Postmarked on 28 OCT 2016   GIC

My Coronado,   *10-26-16*

I hope this letter finds you in good spirits and health. I'm doing good. I know it has been a few days since I got your letter but you know how busy I am. I know that is no excuse but it's only the truth. I'm writing you within the little time I have. I hope you know that I love you no matter how much I don't or do write. You know it's crazy to think that I spent the last 4 years going over my life and how I need to change. I get here and find out I had only gotten to the surface of the problem. It's not fun here at all and it hurts to know things that are not good about yourself. But it will only make me a better person in the end. I'm really excited about getting out of here tho. Time seems to be flying tho. I think it's because our days are the same so you never know when you have woken up in a new one! LOL! :-) Groundhog Day! :-)

Well, my family is doing so good and my kids have written and let me know how excited they are to have me coming home. The two babies (Jack + John) are ready to see me they said. I just can't wait to hold them in my arms. They are so big now! I haven't heard from Gabriel yet but I'm sure he's busy with school. I guess I'm going to have to give him a self-addressed stamped envelope! LOL! I won't have to worry about any of this in a few months! Yeah! So how are the girls? Please send them my love and let them know I think about them all the time. So, you should be going to see your family soon. I know you must be excited. Please let them know I say Hi! Tell them it's a busy life out here being a Navy nurse! LOL! I will be glad to meet them when I'm not so busy! :-)

I look around this room at all these ladies and I wonder how I got myself in this circus! It's like Act One on the right side of the room and then look to your left, here comes Act Two! Man! How did I get here?! I can really say I have learned my lesson! Well, Babe, I want you to know you are the best and I love you so much. We have made it thru some crazy shit! :-) You have really been awesome thru this all. Even when things didn't turn out the way you wanted! :-(I really love you to Pluto and back! Linda has been in touch with me like every day. She is doing really well. She hates the half-way house. She's at it but she will be strong. I miss her more than anyone would ever know! She got her phone yesterday but she hasn't had it set up for me to call yet. I understand because she is just getting on her feet! She's getting a job next week so it must be pretty easy to get a job when you have help from the half-way house! I know I wear a size 7 in jeans! :-) Just need to get down a couple of more sizes and I will be happy. That's if I don't gain more while I'm here! I have been eating like I'm starving and I'm not getting any exercise. So, I may roll out of here! Oh my, I hope not! :-(So please write me and let me know what has been going on in your life. I really need to know! :-) Have you gone hunting yet? For anything? No two-legged anythings please. You need to send me pictures of whatever you get! Well, Babe, my friend said we need to shut the fuck up! She's crazy and a little bored right now. So, she has been blurting out shit to everyone! O.K. I have been helping her. It's so funny to see people look around and wonder where it came from. They think we are so sweet and would never do anything like that. Don't get things twisted. She was just joking! You are not to get mad but laugh! Well, this letter is probably one of the craziest and all over the place letters you have ever gotten from me. I'm sorry but you have no peace. It's nothing but distraction after distraction. I'm trying to stay focused but it's hard. At this moment I feel like I'm at a 300! It's wild and crazy! People going here and people going there. It will be count time in a few and I will need to rack up. I do love you very much and miss you like crazy. I hope to see you in the next few weeks. I know that my sister said something about my nephew coming to visit some time. He's the one that is in college in Austin. We will see. It's nice to know I have family close! I will let you know tho. It's been a very long time since I've seen your face! :-) Your sexy little face is missed by me! Can't wait to see you! I'm sending all my hugs and kisses your way! Remember I love you soo soo soo soo much! Sorry my handwriting is so bad but I have to sit on the top bunk and write or sit in a chair with no table! So please bear with me!

Please take care of yourself! May God bless you with everything you want and need. I'm sending you 10,000 Angels to watch over you and guide you thru each day! Be blessed, Babe! I'm going to go get this in the mail! I bet you will be surprised to get it this fast! I do love you and think about you more than you will ever know! Tons of Hugs + Kisses! Sleep with the Angel! :-)

Yours truly,

Bonnie

I really miss you, Babe!

-xoxoxo-

Postmarked on 05 DEC 2016 GIC

My Coronado, *12-4-16*

 Well, hey there! I just wanted to write to see how you are doing. I'm really just trying to make it one day at a time. It gets really hard to deal with things here because you don't have a lot of time for yourself. I'm not even sure if I thanked you for my Birthday Card! It was truly amazing. By the way, you are the only one who sent me one! :-) So thank you so much for caring and remembering! Not that I would let you forget! LOL! You are really an amazing man. I love you and miss you like crazy. You know it has been forever since I have even touched you and now, you're moving off to another state. I do hope you find a way and the time to come see me before you leave! But I do understand that you have to do what is best for you. I would never want you to stay stuck in a position that would only continue to bring you down. I have been there and I know it's not a good place to be. So, I support you on this move because I know it's what's best for you. I will miss you but I know I will be out soon and we can work things out then. How are the girls taking to this news? I'm sure it's going to break their hearts to be away from you! Please let them know I said hello and they are in my thoughts and I love them! My family has been going thru a lot! My sister-in-law lost her mom last week. She doesn't have any family left but my family! I haven't had mail in a couple of weeks so I don't know what's going on with my kids. I'm just kind of numb about everything right now. I just want to get thru the holidays and get home! Well, Babe, I know this may be short but I just wanted you to know I was thinking about you! I do miss you and love you like crazy! I will call as soon as you can put money on the phone. Until then, just know I love you so, so much and think about you always! Tons of Hugs + Kisses headed your way. Catch them. You don't want to waste any! LOL! You are in my thoughts and prayers. Take care, My love!

Yours Truly,

Bonnie

P.S.

Smile!

Someone cares and loves you!

<u>*2017*</u>

Postmarked on 30 JAN 2017   Burnet, TX

My Coronado,   *1-27-17*

   I just wanted to send you a fast note to let you know what a lucky girl I am to have you in my life! :-) You are truly an amazing man and I love you dearly. You know I have only 40-something days until I am out of here and I'm excited! It blows my mind that I will soon be able to touch you the way I want to or even kiss you the way I want to. It's going to be totally amazing. I will be overwhelmed at first but please work with me! I just found out that I will have an hour layover in Austin at the bus station and then a 5-hour layover at the Dallas bus station. What the heck?! I should arrive in Amarillo at like 3 in the morning. Thank God Christian will be going with me. Oh well, I have to do what I have to do to get home! :-) Well, Babe, I love you very much & I miss you like crazy. I hate it that you didn't get my last letter. So, I hope you get this one. Please let the girls know I said Hi, and they are always on my mind. Please take care of yourself and Thank you very much for all you do. I hope to get to talk to you on the phone soon because you are always working. :-(Well, Babe, know that I love you to Pluto & back and you're always on my mind! I want those songs you printed off! :-)

Just go get a stamp! LOL! Sleep with the angels and dream of me. I will be doing the same. I love you so much!

Yours truly,

Bonnie

P.S.

Tons of Hugs & Kisses headed your way!

I miss you more than you will ever know! Why don't you send me some pictures of you? It's been months since I've seen your face! I really miss you!

Postmarked on 10 FEB 2017   Burnet, TX

My Coronado,   *2-7-17*

Hey there My Love!

I just wanted you to know how much I love you this Valentine's Day. I know we don't get to talk as much as we would like but it's o.k. because we know we love each other even without words. I have had a million things going thru my head about me going home & I don't want for you to think for one second you are not in my plans for the future. I also want to thank you for having enough respect for me to give me the time I need to get my life in order. That says so much about who you are. I really need that in my life. I think you are more than enough for me. I do want you to know that I need your support because I am scared. I'm not scared that I will relapse but I'm scared of the unknown. I do know with you by my side I will get thru it. Babe, I love you so much & I don't want you to ever doubt that. You have been there for me thru some of the hardest times of my life & I'm very grateful. Babe, Have a Wonderful Valentine's Day!

I just got word about my bus trip & I will have a 5hr layover in Dallas. So, I need to ask you to do me a big favor. Can you put like $20 or $30 on my books so that I can have a little cash while I'm at the bus stop to get some food & stuff please? Pretty please with a cherry on top. :-) I would ask my family but I have about drained them because they have bought all my clothes & make-up & stuff for the half-way house! If you can put it on there you can do it thru e-comm & it won't cost as much. Also, you have to put it on there by the end of this month because they close my account 2 to 3 weeks before I leave. They then make me a check out for the amount in my account & I can cash it at the bus stop. I just don't want to leave here without any money. I know I don't ever ask for anything but this is very important. As of today, I have about 38 days before I am out of here! Yeah! I can't wait to be out there & live life again. I *can't wait to spend some real time with you. It's going to be great! Just please bear with me because I did leave my life a mess out there & it's had 4 ½ yrs. to get more of a mess. I can only take it one day at a time, one situation at a time. I just want you to be reassured that I will find time for you. I think I put all the information to the half-way house on the letter that you never received so I'm going to send it again. The number to the girl house you can call whenever & ask for me & if I'm not there it will cost me .50 for each 5 min. phone call. So, I will have to have change to talk. Babe, just know that this is almost over & you will have my nagging ass home to drive you insane. I'm really not sure if you know what you have gotten yourself into. :-) I'm going to go & get this in the mail. I love you with all my heart. I will try to call you this weekend. I will call early so make sure the phone is on. I know I'm a pain in your butt. But that's why you love me! I keep you on your feet! Tons of Hugs & Kisses headed your way!*

Yours always,

Bonnie

Please let the girls know I said hello & I hope they have a wonderful Valentine's Day! Tell them to eat lots of candy for me! ☐

Happy Valentine's Day

My Love!

We didn't have Valentine's Cards so I had to send you this card. I know it's not amazing but it's what I got. I will get to pick my own next year! Love you, Babe!

This is what she wrote inside the Valentine's Card:

My Coronado,

Baby, I just want you to know that my love for you grows more & more each day! I think you're the most amazing man I have ever met! You have stood beside me thru all the years & that says to me what kind of real love you have for me. I just wanted you to know that you are my Valentine's & next year we can spend this day together! I truly love you with all my heart! Happy Valentine's Day!

Hugs & Kisses! Xoxoxo

I hope this Valentines, you know just how much you are loved! I love you to Pluto & back. Now that's lots of love! :-)

Your always,

Bonnie

I love you so much! - ♥ -

Postmarked on 27 FEB 2017   GIC   Burnet, TX

My Coronado,   *Feb 2017*

I wanted to send you this card to wish you the best Birthday ever! I know I have missed out on so many over the years but I can say that after this one, I don't have to anymore! Yeah! I hope your day is as great as you are and you get all you could ever want. I think you are truly amazing & I love you with all my heart. You are very dear to me & I want you to have the best Birthday ever! I would make your day <u>very</u> special if I was there but since I can't be you will have to wait another! I know it sucks but good things come to those who wait!

Xoxoxo Hugs & Kisses

May God Bless you with many more!

Have a Wonderful Day, Babe! I love you to Pluto & back and I miss you more than you could ever know!

Happy B-day to U, Happy B-day to U, Happy Birthday My Coronado, Happy B-day to You

Love always,

Bonnie

Happy Birthday!

From the "Family" & Raul, Casey, Gabriel, Jack, John + Anastasia!

Birthday Blessings

Postmarked on 06 MAR 2017   GIC   Burnet, TX

My Coronado,   *3-5-17*

I just wanted to write you a very important note to inform you just how amazing you are and just how much you are loved by me. :-) Really, I just wanted you to know I think the world of you. You have been there for me for years now & that seems so crazy. How did I find something so great that could love me so much to stick it out with me for so long? You truly are a gift from God & I thank him for you every day. Sometimes I wonder what it is about me that keeps you here. I don't know anyone but you that could love me enough to hold it down for this long. You are so awesome!!!

I'm really kind of upset about my date! :-(I think they just like to get our hopes up so they can break our hearts. But in the end that only makes us stronger & prepares us for the let-downs that life will send our way when we get out of here. I will truly be conditioned to it. Bring it on World! LOL! I'm really relieved that I have a date. It's like I can breathe again! :-) Well, Babe, thank you for being so amazing thru all of this. I couldn't have asked for a better man in my life. I'm going to save the money you put on my books so I will have it when I get out. Thank you so much for doing that. I

113

will put the address to the half-way house at the end of the letter! Send my love to the girls. Well, I'm going to get this in the mail. I love you with all my heart. You truly complete me, babe! Please take care & know you are always on my mind! I love you to Pluto & back!

Yours always,

Bonnie

Amarillo Transitional Treatment House

9300 SE 3ʳᵈ

Amarillo, TX 79118

1-806-398-XXXX

1-806-335-XXXX (Girls House)

Tons of Hugs & Kisses headed your way! I love you!

Postmarked on 22 MAR 2017   GIC   Burnet, TX

Coronado,   *3-20-17*

   I wanted to write you & let you know how much I love you. And I do love you very much. I have missed you like crazy & have felt a little let down when it comes to you. First of all, I have to say that I have never lied to you about anything. I think that has been one of my valuable traits. I have been very real with you & never once have I told you anything just because I thought it's what you wanted to hear. I never ask you for anything because I don't want this relationship to ever be built on anything other than what it's supposed to be built on. But the one time I ask you for anything you promised you will do it, then a few days later you say you did it. Now days later I go to check, expecting to have money for when I go home & money to buy some things I need. And the money you said you sent isn't there. I have to get up and sit in a line at 5:15 in the morning until they call us out. Which just Friday I sit there all day long and never got called out. So, I will have to try again the next time we get to go. Maybe this Friday. So, if I sit there all day, I want to be able to go get what I need when I can

114

because you only get to go about every 3 weeks. So, I say that to say this. Mom put a little bit on my books to go get what I need so I can make it until I leave & I was going to save your money to go get me by on the bus ride home. But I guess now I will do without so I can have money to go home with. I know it's not your place to take care of me & I won't ask you to do anything for me again. I'm sorry I put you in that position to have to lie to me. I wish you didn't feel like you had to lie to me. I thought by now we would have been comfortable with one another to talk things out. I'm really in my feelings about this & I feel very let down. So, know it makes me wonder about other things. I'm not sure what is going on with you but I wish I really knew. I don't want to get out of here in a month & learn all this stuff about you that you could have been honest with me from the beginning. I would have ever judged you or made you feel any less than. I just would like to know why couldn't you just tell me you couldn't afford to right now. Or that you lost your job. Anything but say you did & not do it at all.

Well, I wish this letter could have been more than what it is but I'm just really let down. I hope you can find the time to write back because I wouldn't want to waste any more money on the phone. You tell me you want to do all these things for me when you get out & how are you going to do any of that if you can't do this? You know, I could even see that you would be worried that I would take your money & never have another thing to do with you when I got out. But we have done this for <u>years</u> now. I haven't asked for anything to ever make you believe that to be true. So, what's the deal?? What's the real deal with you? I'm going to be o.k. one way or the other. With or without your help because I know how to survive today. I just hope I haven't wasted all these years on false hopes & wasted dreams. I hope you are everything you have said you were all these years because that's the man I fell in love with. Well, I'm going to end this & get to bed. I still have more weeks to go & I don't want to spend it worrying about tomorrow. All I can do is have faith in God. He has got me thru worse than this. Take care and hope to hear from you soon!

Love,

Bonnie

P.S.

Don't feel like you have to send me anything anymore. I will figure this out. I didn't write this to make you feel like shit so you would send me some money. I wrote it to let you know you let me down & hurt me because you felt you had to lie to me. I'll get past this. Just give me some time! I should have been leaving today & that would have been really messed up to have gotten out thinking I had some money & didn't have shit!

Coronado,   *3-31-17*

    O.K. so I'm not sure what to say here because anyway I say it, will sound like I'm being a spoiled brat or an ungrateful bitch. But let me start out by saying I'm not sure if you really listen when I talk or you don't take in what you are reading when I write. I believe I have been very clear about what I need you to do & why. I feel like if you couldn't do what I asked then you would just plainly & clearly come out & say you couldn't. O.K. When I wrote & asked you to send me like $40.00 on my books for the bus ride because I would be on that trip for 18hrs & I would need something to eat & drink. I told you I wouldn't ask you if I didn't really need it because I don't ever ask for anything. I called later on that week & you told me you had put it on my books so I went to check my account so I could get a few things to last me till I go because I still have 3 weeks left, the money wasn't there. So, I have to call my mom & sister to ask them once again to help me out. I'm really messed up about it because you say you are my man & you want to take care of me but when I ask you to help take care of me, I can't depend on you to do it. If I have to always fall back on my family to get me out of a bind then what do I have you here for? If the tables had been turned you can believe that you would have more than enough. Now, put yourself in my shoes if you can for just one second. We are going to say you have been locked up 4 years plus you have to go thru this treatment center that's 3 times as worse than prison. Then you find out you have to stay an extra month. Now mind you, only in the last couple of years your family has been helping you only with money for you to get what you need. So, you meet someone & y'all fall in love & you're expecting to be with the person when you get out but for some reason, she's not really trying to take care of you, your mind would begin to wonder what is the real deal? Is she broke & don't want to tell you? Is she a millionaire but is a penny pincher? Is she uncertain about the relationship? Or what the Hell?! You have been open about everything & this person has no reason to believe she can't tell you she can't help out because y'all talked this over & it's not going to change how you feel about her. You feel like there's some secret that hasn't been told. Now you're open to just about anything & there's nothing you can't work thru but you just hate this feeling you have. Now you are about to go out into this place called the world after being locked up for 4 1/2 yrs. You haven't eaten or drank anything but the few things they offer at the little store or the chow hall. You're about to experience life again.

    There are so many new things out there that you haven't ever tasted or seen & you will get the opportunity to do so after all these years. You have 18 hrs. before you will be at a place where you will be offered food or drink. Now you think, what am I going *to do? Oh no. I will have to eat & drink something in 18 hrs. So now we are to the point where I asked you for help & you sent $10. O.K. Now I'm going to show you like I'm a bitch. What the hell am I going to do with $10 on a 18hr trip. Can you make it that long with that much money? I'm leaving a place with nothing because I've lost everything I had going out into a world with nothing. I don't want you to feel sorry for me but I would like to think that you would care enough to not let your "so called" girl go out there with nothing. You talk about coming to Amarillo to spend the weekend or to get my hair & nails done. Well, I don't need that bullshit. What I needed was some money to survive on until I could take care of myself. How can you do all this other shit if you can't even help me get home? I just want to know the damn truth for once. You have had years to get ready for me to come home. Years! You say you want this life with me but I don't see any proof. If I'm going to have to rely on my family then I don't need anything extra selling me false dreams. I believe I have given you every chance & doubt in the world. But with this I have no understanding. None! I never ask for shit & I won't ever again. Not to have to feel like this. I should be happy and worry free. Everything should have already been put in place. I'm about to have a second chance to life & I'm not going to spend it begging some man to be the man I need him to be in my life. If I have to rely on my family then I will do that with no extra baggage. I know I can make it out there on my own. I know I can come up fast and have everything I want. But what I don't need is someone that's not truthful about things and continues to set me back when all I ever wanted is for him to prove himself to me So that's your real story before I walk out these doors & find out on my own. Because I will. This is your chance to tell all. I would have been open to help you out in any way possible. You could have been a bum on the streets & I would have loved you thru it. Because love sees passed all that. Some of God's most treasured people are found in prisons & on the streets. You know if you would have been a bum on the streets & you would have told me. That little bit would have meant the world to me. But you have led me to believe that you live a pretty good life & sometimes you struggle but you never struggle enough that you can't take your girls to go do some amazing things you do go out to eat a lot and someone that's down on their luck don't do those things. I know because I did live out there at one time. I just look like this but I'm not dumb one bit. Every game there is to play I have played it. I lived on top of the world and underneath the world. So, what's the one thing that is holding you back? I don't have time for games & I'm not playing them anymore. I'm on to living life in life's terms. I'm about living each day for the blessing it is. I never give up hope & I will always have faith in all but what I won't do is feel the way I feel right now. My account will be closing 2 weeks before I leave. I told you that! That's 14 days before my out date. My out date is on the 24th so subtract 14 days & that means it will be close on the 10th of April! I just wrote Linda to see if she can help me out so just don't worry about it or me. If you had been willing or able to help out you would have by now. You have never given me any reason why you couldn't & I would hate for it to* take all this to get you to help me. We would never make it out there because I would not spend this much time on something. Now I can promise you one thing: I have wasted all this time & it won't change a thing. This is the pattern with you so I will just move on. I know without a doubt in my mind my family & Linda will not leave me out there like that. I know I can count on them. I'm very sorry to have wasted your time over this. What I should have done is not ever asked in the first place. It would have saved a lot of bullshit but it was a lesson learned. I believe you could really be an amazing man if you could learn to be truthful not only to others but yourself. I'm not going to call because I don't want to feel all fucked up these last couple of weeks because this has left me feeling very let down. You have time to write me and let me know what the real deal is. Oh, it's also *so* amazing that I get a J-Pay after months & months of not. I'm just really confused about what you say & what you do. Anyways, you have the floor so give it to me. Let me know what's going on & how you really feel. Time is flying by & before you know it, I will be stepping out these doors. I'm going to go get out of these feelings & go get excited about my release date. Hope you have a wonderful day & I do care enough about you to speak my mind & spend this much time on trying to understand. I will always love you because you have been a bad ass dude in so many ways. I would say that I miss you but it has been so long since I've seen you, it kind of doesn't make sense to say that. Oh, don't come to visit or surprise me because I shut my visits down. Sorry this has to be like this because I really thought things were different. You will always be in my thoughts & prayers. Please take care till I hear back from you.

Sincerely,

Bonnie

P.S.

Smile! Today is a Good day to have a great day!

Thanks for the $10. I will do the best I can with it! I guess something is better than nothing. I am grateful for what I have. Thank you very much!

I just want you to know I'm thinking about my future and I'm really serious about it. I've wasted too much of my life already.

Chapter 8:

Happy Trails

The last reply letter I had written to her was never sent. It remains sealed in an unstamped envelope, but luckily, I saved a copy on my Laptop for me to retrieve and remember what I wrote. It was too late for me to send it as she had already been released and freed to roam this planet, according to any guidelines or restrictions deemed by the Law.

At times I wonder why we found each other in the first place, and the circumstances which allowed us to share this journey together. Did God answer her prayers in sending a messenger to help her continue her onward path towards enlightenment? I certainly felt like there were circumstances beyond my control, and perhaps I was not only in a position to help her because I was preoccupied with saving myself first. I am a better man for knowing her. "It is better to have loved and lost than never to have loved at all" and I found that we are both in a better place now!

Bonnie,

I only sent $10 because the e-comm said I couldn't send any more but that. Your account was approaching its limit.

That is why only $10, Bonnie. I am sorry. That's what I get for trying to follow their online directions. Sorry.

So, here's what has been going on with me, and I feel like I can't give the short story of it so here's the long story:

Once upon a time, I moved in to a house in February 2015.

Since then everything I stored in the bottom floor was ruined due to heavy rains and flooding and mold - paintings, clothes, stuff, etc. Also, the plumbing in the bathroom was not right. I kept calling the landlord to fix the repairs but nothing happened. There is no heat in the house so during the winter time I either slept with a portable heater or slept on the couch at the Lodge. There was no gas so I didn't cook anything. I kept going. I didn't have time to complain.

In February 2017, I found out that my landlord died in August 2016. Well who was cashing my rent checks? The executor to his estate called me and told me that she

119

was selling the house. On March 3, I got a written notice that the house was sold and I told the new owners about all of my issues with the place.

On March 26, I received a notice to remove my belongings from the downstairs within 45 days, after which they will repair the structural and electrical issues and then upgrade the appliances and fix the plumbing issues. After that I will no longer have access to the downstairs and my rent will increase by another $100.

Result: I moved all of my belongings from the house by April 1st, by myself, to avoid staying and living in those conditions. Luckily, I found a storage unit nearby to go back and forth to. During the move I finally disassembled the kitchen table and found your previous note about not receiving the $10 on the table along with some other mail I hadn't opened yet. I felt like crap!

I've been living out of my car since then. I take my showers at the gym I recently joined, and I wear the same clothes once in a while.

Currently, my life is in disarray and my things are either thrown out or in boxes until I start my life again. I Uber here and there and I just started working to pay for food and gas.

I am extremely sorry that I have failed you. The world constantly reminds me of that. I tried doing the best I could but it appears I always come up short. It was not my intention to ever let you down. It seems that my integrity and finances are always in question.

I'm stressed the f&@k out! Only now do I have time to breathe and try to rest my body from it all. I got your last letter today. I stopped by the house to check the mailbox and I got a bunch of mail. A punch in the gut.

No doubt you will succeed. I wish only the best for you as you brave your new world. You don't need any negativity in your life, let-downs or deceit. It appears you felt that way. That is not me. I'm sorry for this illusion that I intended to hurt you or trick you, or waste your time or play games. Good luck on your journey. Perhaps we will meet again on better terms and circumstances. Thank you for everything!

With much love,

Coronado

On Sunday, April 16th, I went to church with my daughters to celebrate Easter Mass and remembered how it felt to congregate in a community setting. As we sat attentively I looked at the Hymn Board to get a jump start on the songs that we would be participating in. It reminded me of the bible verses that Bonnie would periodically include in the bottom of her letters. The priest raised his Bible, the Holy Word, and continued the mass while I sat there thinking about how grateful I was being with my girls, on how I had faith that everything would be all right and felt comfort that it would all work out as it should.

It was time for the Father to perform the transubstantiation and Julianna reached out first and lowered the kneeler. They both knelt beside me, with their hands clasped reminiscent of when they took their first Holy Communion, and we each waited in silence. As others were attentive to the service and partook in the communion, there was another silence that was deafening. I sat at the pew daydreaming about recent events and how things could have been different and how I could heal from the loss of this friendship.

"Let us pray," Father Barker announced.

I wasn't paying attention. I was in an apparent slumber and lost…in thought.

As Veronica slightly kicked my foot, I mistakenly heard her say "Dad, letters pray."

I immediately stood with a grin. "Yes, you're right."

Chapter 9:

The Shoebox

A year and some months later, I revisited my storage unit to make sure nothing was damaged due to regular weather conditions or from Hurricane Harvey, as I had been living on the East Coast since the move, and somehow avoided the disastrous flooding that hurricane had perpetuated in the surrounding areas. Harvey was so devastating that Bonnie actually sent me a text on my phone inquiring if my girls and I were safe from its aftermath.

While dust and some dead insects lay on the floor of the 10 x 20 unit, I couldn't help but to peruse my sole belongings, and that's when, *there*, on a wooden bookshelf next to the Bible and James Joyce, I saw the shoebox that contained all of Bonnie's letters. I didn't realize I still had it amidst the confusion and chaos that occurred prior to its current resting place, but there it was and I was reluctant, at first, to open it.

It was proof that she and I happened, that we were a thing, and she was just as much a part of my Texan experience as anything else. When I eventually opened the lid, not only did a flood of memories lift my spirit and remind me how to feel again, I saw that I actually saved receipts and it was a stark recollection of the price I paid and the cost of my involvement. I sat down on my step stool as I went through the numbers. I continued by tallying the receipts, and I was astonished.

Jpay (2015):	E-Stamps, Monies, etc.	$310.05
Securus Phone line:	6/26/2015 – 3/18/2017	$912.82
E-comm (1/16/2016):	One invoice of Supplies	$38.63
Gas/Transportation:	Visitation of 5 times	$67.20
Food:	Fast Food on Road Trips	$21.17
Postage:	Stamps	$26.50

Here is an actual invoice from January 16, 2016, of items I purchased through the E-comm prison system, and there were restrictions as to how much you can spend during certain periods of time.

122

At the very least, I had spent well over thirteen-hundred dollars, and yet it was far less than any attorney would have charged to get her out of prison, and certainly a fair and considerable price overall as I had the funds at the time and it could have been worse. I was happy to have had the precious letters she had written but that was only half of the story as my letters were mailed to her, and I do not know whatever became of them. They were hers, and these were mine.

At the very bottom of the box, there was a hand-written letter. An unique item, indeed, as it was an original first-draft letter I had written to her, but I sent a copy to her place in Gatesville, TX, instead with better penmanship.

Dear Bonnie,   *6/6/15*

Thank you for taking on Linda's challenge!

Things like this happen to me all the time, and I'm glad for it. You see, little things used to upset me years ago until I realized that 1: only I could control and be responsible for my attitude and actions, and 2: things happen for a reason so accept it, learn from it, and grow above it. Then I picked up on the signs...Life's subtle hints that point me in the right direction. It has pointed me to you. But first...

Howdy, Bonnie Wright. My name is Coronado Borgia. I was born in the states but my family was from the island of Puerto Rico; that makes me a "Boricua". Not that it makes me any more special, but just that I have a certain pride in knowing who I am and where I'm from. I'm forty-three, about two-hundred lbs. wet, and 5'6". I have dark brown eyes but my hair is turning from dark brown to salt and pepper-ish. I guess it's the wisdom and not that I hit my forties. You'll get there and I hope to be at your cake, celebrating with candles, when you do.

I was born in Jersey (New Jersey to non-Jersians) and moved to Houston in June of 2005. Two months later I met Rita – Hurricane Rita. I survived and also with Ike but he was the one who helped me quit smoking. I figured, if it hit the fan I didn't want to pay tons of cash for smokes so I quit cold-turkey. It's easy when I had a "why" and purpose.

And so, I'm a firm believer that books, or literary works, find you so, again, I'm glad that dialogue has opened between the two of us. If you've read this far, you must realize that I'm gonna make you think, for I too have long and challenging stories, but I'm not here for that. Not now, anyway. My job is to make you smile. In hopes that perhaps when you wake in the morning you say to yourself" "This freakin' guy!" but only if I have shared some sunlight into your life in some way.

Thank you for sharing your reason for being there and with that said, I also have no problem with displaying dignity and respect by allowing honesty and not being judgmental. No one is perfect; this we know.

You had asked for a photo of me so I sent only one. If you would like another one of me to put next to your Rembrandt on the wall, I'd be much obliged.

When you get out at the end of this year, what are some of the things you'd do? Do you have someone waiting for you? A man in your life? A husband? Children? What's one thing you miss the most? Do you have a favorite food? Favorite color?

Yes, Bonnie, I would like to get to know more about you, but I don't want to bombard you with tons of questions all at once. I am curious on your photo though. I like your penmanship and I really look forward to hearing from you soon. Please write any chance you get. Maybe you're walking down the hall and you thought of something funny? Please share that with me. Let me be your companion and share those things with me. Random thoughts.

I went fishing this afternoon and thought of you. Wishing you could be with me telling me a story or two over a couple of Cokes. Just a random thought I had while enjoying a beautiful and relaxing day. Could've used a country gal, like yourself, to enjoy it with.

Your friend,

Coronado

www.ingramcontent.com/pod-product-compliance
Lightning Source LLC
Chambersburg PA
CBHW051351280526
45784CB00007B/2906

* 9 7 8 1 0 9 0 2 3 9 8 4 6 *